THE
KINGDOM
WITHIN

✣
✣ *Also by John A. Sanford*

DREAMS: GOD'S FORGOTTEN LANGUAGE

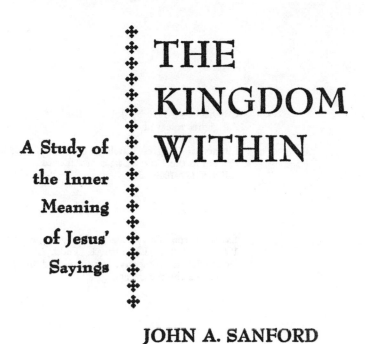

THE
KINGDOM
WITHIN

A Study of
the Inner
Meaning
of Jesus'
Sayings

JOHN A. SANFORD

J. B. Lippincott Company
Philadelphia and New York

Copyright © 1970 by John A. Sanford
All rights reserved
Fifth Printing
Library of Congress Catalog Card No.:77–105548
Printed in the United States of America
ISBN–0–397–10101–5

Excerpts from *The Jerusalem Bible*, copyright ©
1966 by Darton, Longman & Todd, Ltd., and
Doubleday & Company, Inc., are used by permission of the publishers.

Dedicated to the memory of

FRITZ KUNKEL, M.D.

who first introduced me
to the Kingdom Within

Preface

✠✠✠

The truth of Christianity applies to the whole of life, but in our time the Christian message is often proclaimed only in its relevance to the social situation or to the institutional life of the Church. This book is an attempt to balance this outwardly oriented emphasis by showing the inner meaning of Jesus' sayings; that is, their relevance to the unfolding of the whole personality which is within us all. The reader will find here an interpretation of the sayings of Jesus which emphasizes their meaning for his personal, individual life and development. That this is *the* meaning of what Jesus said cannot be proved. That it is *one facet* of the total meaning of Jesus' sayings is indicated, I believe, by the profound insights which Jesus' teachings have for our personal development, as suggested by this book. The teachings of Jesus are like a beautifully cut diamond; they can be viewed from many angles, yet each angle points to the same center. In discussing the inner meaning of Jesus' sayings, I am not claiming that this is the only meaning, but am trying to view the center of Jesus' thought from what is, in our day, an often neglected perspective.

Frequently I shall use case histories in order to elucidate

6

the application of certain of Jesus' sayings to the lives and crises of people today. These case histories are drawn from my own work as a pastoral counselor. In every case the identity of the person involved has been disguised, and permission has kindly been granted to use this situation as an illustration.

The version of the Bible I have used for the quotations is, unless otherwise specified, the Jerusalem Bible, which I favor for teaching purposes because of the clarity, accuracy, and reverence exercised by the translators.

As far as I know the point of view of this book is unusual, for little serious work has been done today to relate the insights of depth psychology to Jesus' sayings. The efforts of Dr. Elizabeth Howes and Dr. Sheila Moon in the San Francisco area are a notable exception, as is the work of the late Fritz Kunkel, to whom I am personally greatly indebted, and whose own book *Creation Continues*, now regrettably out of print, contains many beautiful insights into the message of the Gospels. Anyone who knows Jungian psychology will also recognize my great indebtedness to the psychological work of the late C. G. Jung, which indebtedness I wish to acknowledge, with particular thanks to James Kirsch, M.D., of Los Angeles and Dr. Liliane Frey of Zurich, who have been my "spiritual guides" in recent times. I also want to thank my friend, the Reverend Morton T. Kelsey, who has helped me in many ways. I am deeply grateful for his friendship, his counsel, his suggestions regarding the manuscript, and his own pioneer work in relating Christianity to depth psychology. Such related works of these persons which are published, and a few other works helpful to a general understanding of the New Testament, are included in a brief bibliography at the conclusion of this book.

I also wish to thank the many persons who helped bring the manuscript to completion. I owe a debt of gratitude to my secretary, Mrs. Marie Warnock, for her faithful work, and to Miss Margaret Brown, of St. Paul's Bookshop, San Diego. Especially I want to thank Miss Helen Macey and Mrs. Ruth Budd for their many hours of work in preparing the manuscript for publication; their personal encouragement and hard work have been invaluable to me. Finally, I want to acknowledge with appreciation the members of my Bible seminars at St. Paul's Episcopal Church, San Diego, who helped me work out many insights into "The Kingdom Within."

Contents

✣✣✣

PART ONE

THE
KINGDOM
WITHIN

Introduction

The
Old
Well

✤✤✤

When I was a boy, we spent a month each summer in an old farmhouse in New Hampshire. The house was 150 years old when it first came into our family's hands and had never been modernized. As my father was the minister of a modest-sized Episcopal church, we were always short of money; and so for a long time we lived in the house quite simply, without the benefit of modern plumbing or electricity. Our water supply during these years was an old well which stood just outside the front door. The water from this well was unusually cold and pure and a joy to drink, and the well was remarkable because it never ran dry. Even in the severest summer drought, when others would be forced to resort to the lake for their drinking water, our old well faithfully yielded up its cool, clear water.

Eventually the day came when the family fortunes improved and it was decided to modernize the house. Electricity now replaced the old kerosene lamps, an electric stove took over from the ancient kerosene burner, and modern plumbing and running water were installed. This necessitated a modern well, and accordingly a deep artesian well was drilled a few hundred feet from the house. No longer needed, the old well near the front door was sealed over to be kept in reserve should the occasion arise when for some unforeseen reason the artesian well would not suffice.

So things stood for several years until one day, moved by curiosity and old loyalties, I determined to uncover the old well to inspect its condition. As I removed the cover, I fully expected to see the same dark, cool, moist depths I had known so well as a boy. But I was due for a shock, for the well was bone dry.

It took many inquiries on our part to understand what had happened. A well of this kind is fed by hundreds of tiny underground rivulets along which seep a constant supply of water. As water is drawn from the well, more water moves into it along the rivulets, keeping these tiny apertures clear and open. But when such a well is not used and the water is not regularly drawn, the tiny rivulets close up. Our well, which had run without failing for so many years, was dry not because there was no water, but because it had not been used.

The soul of a man is like this well. What happened to the old well can also happen to our souls if the living water of God does not flow into us. The same is true for the Church; it too can dry up if it does not constantly draw from the living water of God. When this happens, we may suppose that God is dead. God is not dead, and there is living water in abundance, but we are dry, barren, and spiritually dead if we have covered over our souls and ceased to draw up into our consciousness what is contained in the inner depths.

In order to lift water up from a well, it is necessary to have a rope long enough to reach the water. The teachings of Jesus are such a rope. They are the link which we can use to connect us to the depths of ourselves and so to God.

Much of what Jesus said, of course, has already been understood and integrated into our society, so much so that many people suppose they are already thoroughly familiar with the teachings of Jesus and have nothing more to gain from studying them. We have, it is true, understood a great deal of what Jesus had to say about God's intentions for society, and we at least give lip service to Christ's teachings in our social goals. Our Lord said, "Inasmuch as ye have done it unto one of the least of these my brethren, ye have done it unto me" (Matthew 25:40 KJV), and our society is sufficiently Christianized that we make some effort to provide for the less fortunate in our midst. Scholars have also done extensive work on the teachings of Jesus, tracing the historical background of the Gospel records and noting the influence of the early Church. Nevertheless, the significance of the sayings of Jesus for a personal religion, which can guide the individual successfully and meaningfully to a more creative life, has been largely overlooked. It is this personal dimension, the *inner meaning* of Jesus' sayings, to which I wish to call attention in this book.

One of the greatest needs of our age is for such a creative personal religion, for a way through life which will lead to a conscious awareness of God and of His intentions for us, in contrast to the merging of our individual identity with a

collective organization—be that organization relatively benign, like the Church, or malignant, like a totalitarian state.
This need is apparent to the pastoral counselor, who finds
that the outer shells of the personalities of many people
conceal a hollowness, an emptiness longing to be filled,
with an accompanying agony of the soul. It is apparent in
the one-sidedness of much of conventional Christianity, in
the churches of our era which, by concentrating exclusively on extroverted attitudes and ignoring the needs of
the inner man, have created a vacuum which must be filled.
It is apparent in our corporate national and social order as
well. Bereft of a living, inwardly directed religion, men in
their desperation turn to drugs, alcohol, even war, as a
means of escape from their inner isolation, and as a compulsive expression of the sickness within them. The dangerous
alternative to the rediscovery of a personally relevant religion which can lead to greater consciousness of self is the
erection of ever-increasing outer structures to be imposed
on men by the State. Highly structured "isms," such as
Communism, Fascism, or even collective religious movements, move in to fill the vacuum in men's souls. For the
less structure men have within themselves, the more they
will desperately seek to find it outside of themselves.

The rediscovery of the personal and creative side of
Christianity is more possible today than it has been for
many centuries, because of the uncovering of the unconscious. The discovery of the reality of the inner world of
man—of which he is ordinarily unaware, but which greatly
affects his conscious life—is the most important religious
fact of our time and adds great impetus to our search for an
inner Christianity.

The inner world, of course, has been recognized by wise men for a long time. A realization that man's conscious life is grounded upon a secret inner life is at least as old as the prophet Daniel, who reveals his knowledge of the unconscious when he says to King Nebuchadnezzar concerning the King's famous dream,

'O king, on your bed your thoughts turned to what would happen in the future, and the Revealer of Mysteries disclosed to you what is to take place. This mystery has been revealed to me, not that I am wiser than any other man, but for this sole purpose: that the king should learn what it [the dream] means, *and that you should understand* your inmost thoughts' (Daniel 2:29–30; italics mine).

The reality of man's inner world was also known to the men of the New Testament. The demons and angels, principalities and powers, dreams and visions which throng the pages of the New Testament bear testimony to the conviction of the early Christian that man's conscious life was immersed in a sea of spiritual reality. This same conviction that there was a realm of nonphysical reality which men experienced in nonsensory ways continued for several hundred years and dominated the early formative centuries of the Christian faith.*

But within recent times this recognition of the importance of man's inner world has been lost. Reality is thought of exclusively in terms of what can be known through the senses, and man's nature is defined in terms of his will or his

* For a brilliant and comprehensive study of the role of the nonphysical in Christian origins, the reader is referred to the Reverend Morton T. Kelsey's book, *Dreams: The Dark Speech of the Spirit.*

behavior. The New Testament point of view—that man experiences both outer physical reality and inner spiritual reality—is regarded as "mythology," an outdated way of thinking which is irrelevant in a scientific and enlightened era, and which, at best, points only to the faith of the early Church and not to anything objectively real.

This materialistic view of man and negation of New Testament experience has now been challenged by the discovery of the unconscious. At the turn of the century Sigmund Freud succeeded in demonstrating clinically the reality of an inner world of man and its capacity to profoundly affect our conscious states. C. G. Jung has shown that this inner reality is archetypal in nature; i.e., that it has a structure common to all men, and that it cannot be understood exclusively in terms of any individual personal life history. The unconscious is not only the basement of our minds into which we place the discarded material of our own lives; it is also the ocean out of which our conscious lives have sprung, and over which the ships of our souls sail their course through life. No treatment of the inner meaning of Jesus' sayings can be complete which does not take into account the reality of the unconscious, for only an appreciation of the realness of our inner life can return us to something like the New Testament view of man and the world.

At the same time, the sayings of Jesus must not be "psychologized." It would be dangerous to reduce what Jesus has said to anyone's psychological system, and to equate the images of Jesus with the jargon of some particular psychological creed. Even the best psychological system, the most accurate contemporary description of man's psyche, is a historical phenomenon. All concepts, all systems of thought and description are historically conditioned, and are certain to change and evolve as man's knowledge grows. *The beauty of the teachings of Jesus is that they do not depend upon any system of thought,* for Jesus did not express himself by means of jargon or concepts but by means of living images, figures, and parables. In this way he succeeded in freeing his message from history and making it timeless and applicable to all ages. His teachings do not come from man's conceptualized and historically conditioned world, but are drawn from the well of life itself.

In this study of the sayings of Jesus, I will try to preserve the original quality of his teachings. Only a minimum of psychological jargon will be used, for the intent of the book is to lead the reader to his own insights into the nature of Jesus' teaching, and not to pour Jesus into someone's psychological bottle.

Unavoidably, however, a certain theory of personality underlies this work. Briefly stated, it is this: that while man's ego is the center of his conscious life, man also has a vast unconscious life which we can call "the inner world." Here there is a Center to his personality which includes his whole self, while his ego is only the center of his consciousness. This whole self is in each of us as a potentiality, and seeks to be realized in the life process. Our dreams express the urge to the realization of the whole man within us, and give us insight into this inner world of which we are ordinarily unaware. In order for the realization of the whole personality to take place, however, the ego must come into a creative relationship with the inner life, and be constantly expanding in order to give greater and greater expression to the whole scope of the personality.

The use of dream material to illustrate the meaning of

the sayings of Jesus deserves a word of explanation to the reader who is unfamiliar with the symbolic language of the unconscious. Dreams, as Daniel observed to King Nebuchadnezzar,* represent the "thoughts" of our inner mind. While our conscious minds think conceptually, the unconscious expresses itself in the symbolic language of dreams. Often dreams resemble cartoons or parables, or are dramatic representations of inner conflicts or aspirations. But always the dream expresses its meaning through an image, and these images often have an archetypal, timeless quality.

In order to understand a dream, it is best to begin by saying to ourselves, "It is as though . . ." and then go on to the image of the dream, just as Jesus frequently introduces the parables with "the kingdom of heaven is like . . ." and then goes on to the image of the parable. Dreams and the parables both make their point by drawing upon images from the storehouse of the human soul. Dreams and Jesus' teaching are not conceptualized statements, but images in which we may see our own selves reflected. It is for this reason that his parables and sayings speak to the human condition right now as much as they did to the men of his own time.

In my previous book, *Dreams: God's Forgotten Language,* I presented a comprehensive statement of modern dream theory and showed its relevance to the Christian point of view. There will be no attempt to duplicate this work here and, while dream material will be used to illustrate Jesus' message, the reader who is not familiar with the language of dreams will not find it neces-

* See the quotation from Daniel on page 19.

sary to understand the dream-language technically to get the point. Persons who are not aware of their dreams, or recall only fragmentary dreams now and then, may not immediately see the application of the dream material to their own situations, but should not find this a serious obstacle to getting the message of the book. Others, who may be used to the language of dreams and who have recorded their own dreams consistently, will recognize some dream material which resembles their own. Hopefully, my using this material will help them see the further connection between their own inner process and Jesus' message of the kingdom of God.

No one should think, however, that the dreams described in this book are only from disturbed people, or that Jesus' message is only a message for the mentally confused. The people to whose material I allude, always with their permission and anonymously, are no more disturbed than any general sector of our population, and in many cases are persons of unusual intelligence and perceptiveness. There will be much material in this work of interest to the psychotherapist. But the book, as is Jesus' message itself, is primarily addressed to every man who searches for his own wholeness and meaning.

The old well in my family's house in New Hampshire ran dry because no one any longer dropped a bucket into its depths and raised its pure water up into the light of day above. Fortunately, the water of God is limitless, and there is no need for our souls to be dry if we will only lift up from the depths of ourselves the living contents with which God can fill us. This book calls us to lift the cover off our souls, to peer into the depths below, and, using the teachings of Jesus as a rope, to draw upward the timeless, renewing, healing waters of God.

1

The
Personality
of Jesus

✠✠✠

From an ordinary person we can expect only ordinary things. From an extraordinary or unique person we can expect extraordinary things. To get into perspective the sayings of Jesus, we must first determine what sort of person he was. If he differs little from the common run of humanity, we cannot expect to find a hidden depth to his message; but if he proves to be unusual in his personality, we must look for the unexpected in his teachings.

It may seem like an audacious undertaking to try to sketch the personality of Jesus in a meaningful way when this has already been tried many times in more complete texts. Few personalities have been as frequently and variously treated as that of Jesus of Nazareth. In innumerable "Lives of Jesus" many men have described to their own satisfaction what kind of person he must have been, but the gross tendency to oversentimentalize Jesus and the ease with which we can project into the figure of Jesus our own idealized images raise the question as to whether it is possi-

ble to talk of a personality of Jesus at all. Add to this the
paucity of the Gospel records, the complete lack of any
physical description, and the debatable nature of some of
the passages, and the task may look hopeless.

On the other hand, the basic historicity of the personality of Jesus cannot be doubted. Not only do we have the
recorded events of the Gospels—no mean historical data as
ancient documents go—but we have the very existence of
Christianity as a testimonial to the existence of a remarkable
person who launched a radical and enduring new religion.
It is not that we are without grounds, then, for believing
that there was a person called Jesus of Nazareth, nor are we
devoid of facts about him; the difficulty has been in finding
some kind of yardstick by means of which an accurate
sketch of his personality may be made.

Fortunately, we now have such a yardstick. The late
Swiss psychiatrist C. G. Jung devoted most of his life to the
description of the whole, or total, man. He has given us
certain categories by means of which the range of personality may be described. It is valid to take Jung's insightful
description of what makes up man's totality and apply these
categories to what we know of Jesus of Nazareth. The
results are most interesting and revealing.

Jung's most basic category is that of *extroversion* and
introversion. The extrovert's center of interest and sense of
personal identity are found in the world outside of himself;
here is where he finds what is most appealing and valuable
to him. The introvert, on the other hand, ultimately meas-
ures his values by what is taking place within him, and finds
that his chief interests and sense of identity lie in his inner
world. Most people are well developed in one area of life at

the expense of the other. So the extrovert functions quite well as long as life calls upon him to deal only with outer realities, but falls into confusion if he is forced within himself. The introvert may be quite at home with his own inner realm, but feels overwhelmed by the world outside of himself. A whole person, however, has achieved some development in both realms. Without some development within himself, the life of the extrovert may be shallow; without some capacity to function in the world, the insights of the introvert may prove ineffectual. Only if a person has some development both inwardly and outwardly can he be said to approach wholeness.

When we apply these categories to Jesus of Nazareth, we find that he appears to be equally developed in both the extroverted and introverted realms. We see his extroverted development in a life which involved him with people. Jesus met people constantly and confronted them both individually and in large crowds. In the Gospel of Matthew alone we read of twenty-four separate encounters between Jesus and a large multitude. Such a capacity for outgoing relationships, for functioning competently in the world, is a characteristic of extroversion. At the same time, however, Jesus' introversion is equally well developed. Often we read that he retires alone in order to pray (e.g., Luke 5:16). He initiates his ministry with forty days of solitude in the wilderness (Matthew 4:1–2/Mark 1:12–13/Luke 4:1–2), something which no extrovert would think of doing. At crucial moments in his life he retires into solitude again in order to reorient himself and discover his inner direction, as, for instance, in the Garden of Gethsemane prior to his arrest and crucifixion (Matthew

26:36–46/Mark 14:32–42/Luke 22:40–46). It would be impossible from the evidence of the Gospels to say that Jesus was an extrovert or an introvert; the only conclusion we can draw from the Scriptural evidence is that he was both.

A second set of categories by means of which Jung describes wholeness is the four functions of the psyche. In addition to being either extroverted or introverted, Jung says, the ego orients itself to life by means of four basic psychological functions. Two of these functions, *thinking* and *feeling*, have to do with arriving at conclusions. Two others, *sensation* and *intuition*, have to do with perception, or the gathering of information. These four functions are of such a nature that the development of any one of them is ordinarily possible only at the expense of its opposite, so that we may represent the four functions schematically like this:

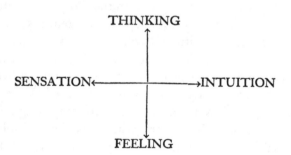

Let us take a look at the strengths and weaknesses of each of these functions. The person whose thinking function is well developed is called a "thinking type." His may be either extroverted or introverted thinking, depending on which is his basic orientation. As a thinking type he is at his best in dealing with situations which can be resolved through a process of abstract thought or conceptualization. He will be at his worst in a situation which requires him to feel rather than to think.

A feeling-type person, on the other hand, will be quite at home with his feeling life, and by means of it will be able to arrive at accurate and meaningful value judgments. His feelings are more than emotions. They function as a sure guide to what is truly valuable and important in life, and imbue him with the capacity for commitment and loyalty. Where a situation calls for this kind of orientation, such a person is at his best; but where a thinking process is called for, he is caught on his inferior side.

The sensation function has been called the "reality function," for this is the function which leads to awareness of the facts of a situation, especially the facts of a situation in the physical world. Sensation-type people are often eminently practical, very much aware of the information which their senses bring them, and well oriented to the business of practical living.

They are a contrast to the intuitives, for the intuitive function brings information of the inner world, the world of shadows or intangibles. The intuitive function has been defined as "unconscious perception," or "seeing around corners." Thus both the sensation type and the intuitive type are strong on *perceiving*. But while the sensation type perceives facts brought to him by his physical senses, the intuitive type perceives the subtler, more elusive facts of relationships or of the psyche, and, if he is extroverted, of possibilities in the outer realm.

The fact that people have different psychological functions accounts for many areas of disagreement. Take the Vietnam war as an example. A sensation type will be intrigued by the *facts* of the situation, and will gather much information regarding the country's present condition. The intuitive type will be more interested in the history of the situation and in the underlying psychological and historical reasons for the conflict. The thinking type will attempt to arrive logically at a positive stand regarding the war, perhaps relying on a syllogism like "All communism is evil and a threat to the United States. Evil must be stamped out. Therefore, the Vietnamese communists must be defeated." The feeling type, however, will arrive at the value of the situation by *feeling*. His reaction of "isn't the war terrible?" may lead him to a position quite contrary to that of the thinking type. Obviously a *whole* appreciation of the situation will require the viewpoint of all four functions.

This whole standpoint, however, is difficult to achieve, for as the ego (the center of our conscious personality) develops, it tends to use whichever of these four functions works best for that particular personality. Which function it is may depend largely upon heredity, although environmental factors also play their role. Sometimes a second function is also partially developed in addition, forming a sort of auxiliary. The other functions, largely neglected, fall into the unconscious, where they are known as the "inferior functions," in contrast to the "superior functions" which are well developed and adapted for the use of the ego. For some time in life the ego may function satisfactorily by means of the one or two superior functions, but ultimately, if wholeness is to come about, some measure of growth must take place in the other functions as well.

Frequently this integration of the inferior side becomes a necessity if the personality becomes so one-sided that the unconscious establishes a troublesome counterposition.

This is a very brief sketch of a complicated and rich part of psychology, but perhaps it is enough to enable us to apply these categories to the personality of Jesus.

The sensation function is the so-called "reality" function; it brings us information about the facts of our world. In Jesus we can see a well-developed sensation side in his acute awareness of the facts of the world in which he lived. In his teachings and parables he uses everyday examples such as a grain of mustard seed, or the sower sowing his seed, or the woman searching for a lost coin. He is no other-worldly visionary, but a man rooted in the reality of this world. He is also familiar with the power structure of his society. He knows the worldly facts of life, who has the power, and how the power structure works. No one would ever have thought of saying of him that he was unrealistic or impractical. All of this is the mark of a man with a well-developed sensation function.

On the other hand, his intuitive function is equally well developed. This is clear from his immediate contact with the inner world, his use of images, and his sensing of unseen realities not visible to the senses but known to the inner vision. His intuition also gives him a keen insight into men's souls (Matthew 22:18, John 6:15, Luke 9:47, Mark 2:8, Luke 20:23). So John can write of Jesus' understanding of men,

> but Jesus knew them all and did not trust himself to them; he never needed evidence about any man; he could tell what a man had in him (John 2:24–25).

The thinking function of Jesus is seen in his intellectual bouts with the Pharisees, and in his astuteness. When confronted with a situation which called for quick logical analysis, for objective and keen thought, Jesus met the situation with ease, the sign of a well-developed thinking person. At the age of twelve, we learn, he sat among the learned doctors in the Temple (Luke 2:41–50). At the close of his life we find him engaged in battles of wits with the Pharisees, who seek to trap him into all kinds of difficulties only to be outwitted by a man capable of keen abstract conceptualization (cf. Matthew 22:15–22/Luke 20:20–26/Mark 12:13–17; or Matthew 22:23–33/Mark 12:18–27/Luke 20:27–40; or Matthew 22:41–46/Mark 12:35–37/Luke 20:41–44).

The feeling function results in accurate realizations of values; it is the evaluative function par excellence. If thinking tells what a thing is, feeling tells us its value. From a realization of values come many compassionate, or indignant, responses to people and to life situations. Examples of Jesus' feeling function abound in the Gospels. Twelve times, for instance, we read that Jesus was "moved with compassion" for people in various kinds of distress. In this he shows the great value which he places on individual life. Also, in his encounters with the Pharisees he repeatedly places the humanness of a situation above the Law, stressing the highest value. A statement such as "Set your hearts on his kingdom first, and on his righteousness, and all these other things will be given you as well" (Matthew 6:33) is an illustration of the strongly evaluative feeling function of Jesus at work. Even his cleansing of the Temple (John 2:13–22, Matthew 21:12–13, Mark 11:15–17, Luke 19:45–

46) illustrates his strong sense of value, as does his occasional righteous anger.

The picture we get, therefore, is of a man well developed in all four functions. It is not possible to isolate any one of the functions of Jesus as an inferior one, for examples can be drawn showing good development in each. It is as though in the personality of Jesus we are seeing a whole person. But let us look still further.

Another important area of wholeness for a person lies in the development of both the *feminine* and *masculine* potentials. The masculine aspect of personality may be variously described as logos, or outgoing reason, active creativity, controlled aggressiveness, psychological firmness, the capacity to strive for goals and overcome obstacles en route. The feminine aspect of personality comprises eros, or the capacity for relationships, understanding, awareness of others, creativity through receptiveness, an indirect way of attaining goals, patience, compassion, the valuation and nourishing of life. Now everyone, man or woman, contains possibilities for both masculine and feminine development, and no one can approach wholeness without some development in both areas. A person who is developed only in the masculine area will be brutal rather than aggressive, intellectual in a sterile, academic way rather than a man possessing logos, and his undeveloped feminine side will show itself as moodiness, pettiness, and irritability. A person who is developed only in the feminine area will be weak rather than receptive, overly sensitive rather than capable of deep relationships, while the undifferentiated masculine side will show up as inner stubbornness rather than firmness, opinionatedness rather than reason.

In the case of Jesus there is equal development in both masculine and feminine areas. To begin with the masculine side, Jesus was a fighter par excellence. He carried the battle resolutely to his enemies and, though his struggle was spiritual rather than physical, it required no less of a capacity for expressing masculinity. He was direct with people, confronting both friends and enemies directly and firmly. He moved resolutely toward the goals he had in mind. The story of the cleansing of the Temple is a good example of his ability to control aggression. His capability of clear logos is apparent in his dialogues with the Pharisees and in his teachings, which were immediately recognized as having authority.

In the feminine area we find that, unlike John the Baptist, Jesus was a friend of women. In fact, there is no instance in the Synoptic Gospels of any woman who was ever his enemy. Such an appreciation of women is always a sign of a well-developed feminine side. He was deeply in touch with the life process, as is seen in his use of nature illustrations for his parables. He was close to children, another sign of a good feminine development. His eros development is shown in his capacity for extraordinarily deep personal relationships, and, most supremely, in his final great act of caring on the Cross.

Here too, in the masculine-feminine areas, we find a man of balanced development, a man who was whole.

Another area of development necessary for wholeness is the development of a strong *ego;* that is, a conscious personality capable of exerting itself effectively in life. A person with a strong ego is able to cope with, adapt to, or overcome life situations. A person with a weak ego, on the other hand, is not able to cope with life and as a substitute erects defenses around himself, or relies on various neurotic devices. Out of this comes the egocentricity so dangerous to our relationship with God.

The strength of Jesus' human ego is apparent in his capacity to conceive of and carry through his extremely demanding life task, involving as it did his ultimate renunciation of himself. Only a person with a strong ego can give up his ego; we cannot give to God what we do not possess. The figure of Jesus going alone and voluntarily to the Cross for the sake of his mission is the figure par excellence of a man of tremendous ego strength. But ego strength is not egotism. The man with a strong ego is the one who can live for the Higher Will within himself, turning his life over to a Power still stronger than that of his human will. This we see in Jesus in his complete dedication to fulfilling the mission which God set before him. Precisely because his ego was strong, the will of Jesus was constantly subordinated to the Higher Will which he knew was to rule his life.

Looked at psychologically, the Gospels reveal the personality of a whole person. It is apparent that we have here in Jesus of Nazareth the paradigm of the whole man, the prototype of all human development, a truly individual person, and therefore someone unique.

This uniqueness accounts for Jesus' freedom from historical conditioning. No ordinary man escapes the historical and psychological conditioning of his thoughts, personality, and attitudes by the history and the collective psychological atmosphere of the people of his time. All of us are born into history at a particular time, with a historically conditioned mentality and psychology which, to a large degree, inevitably determine our insights, influence our ideas, and shape our personality. Many persons have attempted to find the current attitudes of Jesus' time which might have influenced his personality and teaching. But a remarkable thing about the personality of Jesus is that such historical conditioning is not in evidence. The personality and the teachings of Jesus are not inherited from the collective spirit of his time, but stand out in contrast to it. Their very uniqueness is a testimony to the reality of his personhood.

One great struggle of his time, for instance, was the conflict between the spiritual and the physical. The men of his day could be divided into those who favored the spiritual side and repressed or denied their physical side, and those who lived for their passions and appetites and denied their moral and spiritual character. John the Baptist, for instance, lived out his spiritual side, but not his material, physical side, for which he won the enmity of women, since women are often more rooted in the natural side of life than are men. St. Paul, great man though he was, also never entirely solved this split between the spiritual and the material sides of man and, like John the Baptist, favored a somewhat ascetic approach to life. Jesus, however, was no ascetic. There is not a passage in the Gospels in which he favored the denial or negation of the bodily, instinctive side of man. To the contrary, it was said of him that he was a glutton and a drunkard (Matthew 11:19, Luke 7:34), so shocked were people at how he, appearing as a man of God, could live without denying his appetites.

In the attempt to trace historical connections between

Jesus and other groups, various cults or sects have been suggested as Jesus' historical antecedents. But none of them fit the facts. While Jesus was a good Jew, for instance, his teachings departed so radically from the Judaism of his day that we cannot entertain the idea that he acquired his insights from the Jewish collective thinking of his time. Others have attempted to show that Jesus was an Essene, and owed his teachings to this widespread group made especially famous in recent years by the Dead Sea Scrolls. But there is practically nothing in the teachings of Jesus which parallels the teachings of the Essenes, and his denial of asceticism makes it impossible to consider him as related to them, for they were noted for ascetic practices. It seems that Jesus acquired his insights from a direct contact with a numinous * power; that is, from God. The story of the Transfiguration illustrates the direct contact Jesus had with such a numinous *inner authority*, as does the story of his baptism.

Jesus' personality and teachings are unique and not historically conditioned because they do not stem from a human source, but are rooted in his consciousness of the inner world through which comes his awareness of the holy God whom the prophets before him had known in part. From this came his individual consciousness, which eventually destroyed the collective, formalized religious structure of his time. In *this* sense Jesus renews the spirit of Israel, the

---

* The word "numinous" was coined by Rudolph Otto (*The Idea of the Holy*) and was used extensively by C. G. Jung to refer to the feeling we have when confronted by a spiritual reality other than a human being like ourselves. If we saw a ghost, an angel, or a direct manifestation of holy or unholy power, we would experience an awed creaturely response to a numinous power.

wrestler with God,* in that he bears in his consciousness
the numinous will of the heavenly Father.

Such a personality must have existed, for he could never
have been invented. No doubt there are many places where
the early Church has influenced the Gospel records, and we
should read the Gospels with all the historical criticism we
can muster. But the ultimate personality of Jesus cannot be
doubted because it could not have been contrived. The
testimony of psychology is that Jesus of Nazareth existed,
and that the Gospel records are essentially accurate, because Jesus' personality is unique.

If in Jesus of Nazareth we have a personality who was
whole and unique, we shall not be wrong in supposing that
the teachings of such a man will also be unique. The trouble with most interpreters of Jesus' message is that they
have not been prepared for this uniqueness; they have tried
to reduce his message to historically conditioned ideas, and
so have missed much of the depth of what he said. As we
proceed now to look at what Jesus said regarding the kingdom of God, we must keep in mind the uniqueness of his
personality. Then our minds may be open to his message;
we can avoid the danger of those who try to contain the
mind of Jesus in a limited framework, and can let our own
minds be expanded by his original and timeless insights.

* Genesis 32:24–28.

2

The Treasure of the Kingdom of God

✤✤✤

In the thirteenth chapter of Matthew's Gospel we find two brief parables which point to the paradoxical heart of the mystery of the kingdom of heaven. A look at their inner meaning will open the door to this mysterious reality which was so central to Jesus' teaching.

'The kingdom of heaven is like treasure hidden in a field which someone has found; he hides it again, goes off happy, sells everything he owns and buys the field' (Matthew 13:44).

For reasons which we shall look at more closely in a moment, Jesus always talks of the kingdom of heaven in an image or figure. Here the figure is that of a treasure hidden in a field. The kingdom is, therefore, something of great value, which, in this parable, the individual may discover. Once someone has found this treasure, he recognizes it to be so valuable that he gives up everything else he has in order to acquire it.

There is an inner reality within each of us which is like a great treasure lying hidden in the field of our soul waiting to be discovered. When someone finds this inner treasure, and recognizes its value, he happily gives up all other goals and ambitions in order to make it real in his life.

Now let us compare this with the second parable.

'Again, the kingdom of heaven is like a merchant looking for fine pearls; when he finds one of great value he goes and sells everything he owns and buys it' (Matthew 13:45–46).

At first glance it looks as if this parable duplicates the parable of the treasure. But, as Fritz Kunkel has pointed out,* in the first parable the kingdom is a treasure which *we* search for and find; in the second parable the kingdom is likened to a merchant who is searching for things of value. In this case *we* are the pearls, found by the kingdom of God.

So the paradox is that the kingdom is both that which we find within ourselves as an inner treasure, and also that which is searching to find us, who when found become something of supreme value in the eyes of God. *We* are the fine pearls if the kingdom can take root within us, and to such a person God gives a place of supreme value in His creation.

* *Creation Continues.* page 193.

Very often in the history of Christianity theologians and teachers have dwelt upon the unworthiness of man, his proneness to sin, his worthlessness in contrast to God's supreme goodness; they have even laid the responsibility for evil at man's doorstep. There is none of this in the teachings of Jesus. Jesus is often disappointed in men, of course, but only because man is potentially of the highest value, the inheritor of God's very own kingdom. He harbors the kingdom within his own soul. God searches for the man who will recognize the kingdom within him, and He ascribes to such a man supreme value.

The importance of the kingdom of heaven is apparent from even a cursory reading of the Gospels. It is the central arch of Jesus' teachings, being found in Mark's Gospel thirteen times, in Luke's twenty-eight times, and in Matthew's thirty-eight times. In John's Gospel it occurs as an expression only once, but John uses the equivalent expression "eternal life" with much the same meaning. Fifteen of the parables of Jesus are directly concerned with the kingdom of God, and in Matthew alone twelve of his parables are introduced with the expression, "The kingdom of heaven is like. . . ." It is apparent that if we know what Jesus meant by the kingdom of God we shall be in possession of the key to his teachings, for everything he said is directly or indirectly related to it.

This importance of the kingdom of God has not gone unnoticed by scholars and theologians, and volumes have been written on the subject. Almost all these efforts suffer from two great drawbacks: the determined effort made to relate Jesus' ideas of the kingdom of God to prevailing ideas already in existence before his time; and the materialistic point of view of the various scholars, which has blinded them to the kingdom as an inner, spiritual reality. It is only when we have recognized the uniqueness of Jesus' consciousness, and the importance and reality of man's inner world, that we can properly appreciate the significance of the kingdom of God in Jesus' teachings and in our lives.

We do not find these limitations, however, in the early Church. The early Fathers of the Church knew that man experienced both outer physical reality, of which he became aware through the senses, and inner, spiritual reality, known to him directly, intuitively, through the soul and in personal experiences such as dreams and visions. The kingdom was not something coming upon man from outside of himself, but was a reality within himself, the very foundation of his personal existence, and something which could be experienced by the individual.

The kingdom of God as a spiritual reality within men must be described as a psychological reality insofar as it is experienceable by the individual in the development and unfolding of his personality. When we find and realize the kingdom in ourselves, we experience a growing wholeness, an increasing sense of the meaning of our individual personality, a realization of new and creative energies, and an expanding consciousness. This leads us beyond our individual ego-existence to an experience with a transcendent source of life, and to a creative life in the social sphere. The kingdom involves the realization of our personalities according to the inner plan established within us by God; hence, the unfolding of a Self which predates and transcends the ego. It is in this light that we shall now take a

closer look at some of the things Jesus said about the kingdom of God.

When Jesus talks about the kingdom of God, he always
does so, as we noted above, in images or figures. He never
says, "The kingdom of God *is* such and such," but always,
"The kingdom of God is *like* such and such." The most
prevalent way of expressing these images is by the parable.
The frequent use of the parables did not escape the notice
of the disciples, who once asked Jesus, "Why do you talk
to them in parables?" Jesus replied,

> 'Because the mysteries of the kingdom of heaven are re-
> vealed to you, but they are not revealed to them' (Matthew
> 13:11/Luke 8:10/Mark 4:11).

Now Jesus is not being deliberately obscure in using
images when he could speak plainly. Rather, the disciples,
through their close contact with Jesus and their growing
spiritual awareness, have already glimpsed this reality
which Jesus calls the kingdom. But the multitudes have not.
Their eyes must be opened to inner reality. Such an "open-
ing of one's eyes," a "revelation," can never be given directly in so many words. We see inner reality only through
an "aha!" experience, a sudden insight into our own being.
There is no way to describe inner reality directly; we can
only hope to lead people into a perception of it. Jesus
knows this, and his parables are designed to lead people into
an insight of the kingdom. So he gives them a figure; and if

they see the inner meaning of the figure, they will begin to see the reality of the kingdom.

This is why Jesus calls the kingdom "a mystery." The Greek word for this is "mysterion." A "mysterion" was something to be known, but it was an initiated knowledge which a person could acquire only through his own individual insight and experience, and which could not be communicated through an ordinary educational process.

Our dreams are close to this same reality which Jesus called the kingdom. Like the parables, dreams speak in figures and are understood only through a sudden insight, an "aha!" experience which opens our eyes to a facet of our being of which we were previously unaware.

One of the most important images Jesus used to describe the kingdom is the *image of growth*. While this image occurs in many places (cf. Matthew 13:4–9, 24–30; 7:15–20), the best-known examples are in the two following parables:

> 'The kingdom of heaven is like a mustard seed which a man took and sowed in his field. It is the smallest of all the seeds, but when it has grown it is the biggest shrub of all and becomes a tree so that the birds of the air come and shelter in its branches' (Matthew 13:31–32/Mark 4:30–32/Luke 13:18–19).

> 'The kingdom of heaven is like the yeast a woman took and mixed in with three measures of flour till it was leavened all through' (Matthew 13:33/Luke 13:20–21).

In the case of the Parable of the Mustard Seed the image is of something which begins as a small, seemingly insignificant thing, but which, through a process of growth, achieves great strength and stature. (In the Orient the "mustard tree" is quite a large tree.) So the kingdom of heaven begins in a man's life as something seemingly small and insignificant, but through a process of growth becomes a mighty power. The image of the tree is appropriate, for just as a tree is rooted in the earth but reaches up to heaven, so the unfolding of personality includes both our earthy and spiritual natures.

In the case of the Parable of the Yeast, yeast is what causes a loaf of bread to rise. It is seemingly insignificant in itself, yet without yeast the bread remains flat and unfinished. So the kingdom of heaven is the reality in a man's life which causes his whole personality, and the outer fabric of his life as well, to achieve completeness.

Those familiar with the workings of the unconscious recognize a process at work within the individual constantly seeking to bring about that person's wholeness and fulfillment. This inner growth potential is regarded by most people as small, insignificant, and valueless, while the important things are said to be outside of ourselves. Yet it is through the acceptance of the inner power for growth that our lives rise and become fulfilled. It is not surprising in view of this to find that our dreams often reflect this inner growth under the image of a great tree, or stress the importance of a child, who also frequently represents our growth potential. A conventional, narrowly scientific attitude toward man cannot take into account man's potential for growth, for it sees only man's outward behavior and is blind to his potential selfhood. A religious psychology has the insight to see that man is not truly himself until his life has been completed, and that this completion involves a growth which, like a mustard seed, begins as something very small, but becomes great and, like yeast, comes to permeate his whole life.

Because the kingdom is associated with the inner growth of the individual, it is very much *a here-and-now experience.* While Jewish apocalyptists before him projected the kingdom of heaven into the future and saw it as a great event coming upon man from outside, Jesus saw that the kingdom of heaven begins within a man, and is initiated in this present time. It is also in the future because, although it is here now as a potentiality influencing life, its realization is not complete. So Jesus can say,

> 'the kingdom of heaven is close at hand' (Matthew 4:17, 10:7, and many parallels).

And in John's Gospel Jesus says to Nicodemus,

> 'Except a man be born again, he cannot see the kingdom of God' (John 3:3 KJV).

This certainly implies that the kingdom is a present reality to be entered into by the individual when he achieves such a radical transformation of his character that it is represented under the image of rebirth.

There is also an interesting emphasis on the here-and-nowness of the kingdom in the Lord's Prayer. Jesus tells us to pray "Thy kingdom come," stressing the need to reach for the kingdom's realization. But he also adds that we should pray "Give us this day our daily bread." The word rendered "daily" in English is a translation of a very unusual Greek word. In fact, the Lord's Prayer is the only place where this word occurs in the Bible, and elsewhere quite a different word is used for a "daily" occurrence of some sort. Recent evidence from the Dead Sea Scrolls indicates that this word rendered "daily" applied to a special meal partaken of by the devout for religious purposes. The early Church Fathers used this special word to refer specifically to the Eucharistic food. So the "daily bread" is no ordinary bread, but living spiritual food to be taken into ourselves in the here-and-now so that we may be prepared for the imminent reality of the kingdom.

Jesus was able to preach the imminent presence of the kingdom because man's spiritual and psychological development was now such that he could arrive at a new stage of his potentiality. For the first time the individual man could achieve an inward relatedness to God. While the religion of the priests and prophets before him had been largely a matter of the relationship of God to his people, the new expression of this faith which Jesus gives us is that each individual is to achieve his own relatedness to God. In this way the individual participates personally in the kingdom, which he is now ready to receive. For the individual today the kingdom is achieved through the process of inner growth into his own wholeness and creativity.

From all this it is clear that the kingdom is *a very personal reality*. God has prepared the kingdom for the individual, who may enter it in this lifetime and will discover the kingdom to exist within himself. So Jesus says in two controversial passages:

'the kingdom of God is within you' (Luke 17:21 KJV)

and

> 'You must therefore be perfect just as your heavenly Father
> is perfect' (Matthew 5:48).

The passage from Luke 17:21 would seem to clearly
refer to the kingdom as an inner reality except for the confusion regarding the Greek preposition rendered in this
King James translation as "within." The preposition in
question can also mean "among," and has been so translated
by almost all the modern translators of the Bible in prefer-
ence to the traditional "within." This choice of translation
betrays the extroverted attitude of our time which finds it
hard to conceive that anything worthwhile could be within
us. In the early Church, however, this preposition was
invariably rendered "within." Being closer to Jesus' time,
the Fathers were also closer to his spirit and knew of the
reality of the inner world.

In the second phrase the difficulty for the English reader
hinges on the word "perfect." This implies to most modern
men the idea of a one-sided pureness; that is, a person
without any kind of thought or emotion which could be
regarded as in any way sinful or wrong. The Greek, however, means literally "brought to completion" or "brought
to the end state." If we understand the word in this way,
we see that Jesus is urging us to be brought to the end state
for which we were created and which is brought about
through the unfolding of the inner self. This also throws
light on the ancient problem, "How can God, the transcendent Creator of the universe, also be a personal reality
for the individual?" The answer is that He is as personal to
us as our own inner creative process.

Although the kingdom is highly personal to the individual, it is nevertheless potentially *open to all men*. The kingdom knows of no barriers of race, creed, sex, or social status. While the Gospels suggest that Jesus might have gone through some deep personal probing of his own before he came clearly to this recognition (cf. Matthew 15:21–28, the story of the Canaanite woman), nevertheless Jesus states unequivocally,

> 'many will come from east and west to take their places with Abraham and Isaac and Jacob at the feast in the kingdom of heaven' (Matthew 8:11/Luke 13:29).

And again in the Parable of the Wedding Feast, which represents the kingdom of God, the king orders his servants,

> 'go to the crossroads in the town and invite everyone you can find to the wedding' (Matthew 22:9/Luke 14:23).

Those who have been given the opportunity to observe the universal nature of the structure of man's inner world will have no trouble understanding why the kingdom is available to all men. Just as there is a universality of form to the human body, so there is a universality to the inner man. The same typical (archetypal) structures are found in men everywhere, and express themselves through their inner imagery. The Greek philosopher Plato would have ascribed this to the fact that all men are replicas of the Universal Man, the Idea of Man in the Mind of God. In the Old Testament each man is created in the image of God. In Christian language it is the universality of Christ in all men. For Jesus it is the call of the kingdom to each person. To the psychologist it is the archetypal structure of the human mind, and the universality of the urge to wholeness.

The paradox is that this universality of the kingdom does not in any way invalidate the uniqueness of the individual. The kingdom always finds a unique expression in each person because the kingdom is the creativity of life expressed in a person, and this creativity yearns for uniqueness. But underlying the uniqueness is the universal call.

This brings us to the *highly moral life* required for entrance into the kingdom. Only the individual with a differentiated moral consciousness—i.e., one who leads his life by an individually worked out set of values based on self-knowledge—can enter into the kingdom of God.

'For I tell you, if your virtue goes no deeper than that of the scribes and Pharisees, you will never get into the kingdom of heaven' (Matthew 5:20).

The morality of the scribes and Pharisees consists in following rules and regulations which seek to govern a man's actions in every conceivable circumstance in life. When Jesus calls upon those who would enter into the kingdom to exceed this morality of the scribes and Pharisees, it is not that he wishes to overthrow this body of Law, but to transcend it.

'Do not imagine that I have come to abolish the Law or the Prophets. I have come not to abolish but to complete them. I tell you solemnly, till heaven and earth disappear, not one dot, not one little stroke, shall disappear from the Law until its purpose is achieved' (Matthew 5:17–18/Luke 16:17).

could one say 'until its purpose is achieved in the one who follows the law – when the law has lifted one into real consciousness, its purpose is achieved & it can disappear – one's morality will then be a matter of inner fidelity to the spirit rt fidelity to a set of rules'

The kingdom requires a morality which is not founded on rules and regulations imposed from outside, but on self-knowledge. This self-knowledge can be achieved through inner confrontation. The inner confrontation occurs when we confront the person within us for whom the Law is necessary. It would not be necessary to have a Law forbidding murder, adultery, stealing, coveting, and slander if there was not a part of our personality which might do exactly these things. The scribes and Pharisees seek to avert the danger of this inner "shadow" by following rules which prohibit these things. But the higher morality requires confronting the shadowy one within us who has made the rules necessary in the first place. In this way we achieve a truly differentiated moral attitude toward ourselves and life and are fit for the creative life of the kingdom.

This *need for self-confrontation* for those who would belong to the kingdom is of paramount importance to Jesus. We find it in his first utterance,

'Repent, for the kingdom of heaven is close at hand' (Matthew 3:2).

and in such shocking statements as this one to the Pharisees,

'I tell you solemnly, tax collectors and prostitutes are making their way into the kingdom of God before you' (Matthew 21:31).

The Pharisees were the most meticulous persons in the entire community in keeping the Law. But precisely because of their success in this, they were convinced of their own righteousness, and therefore failed to see their inner "shadow" side. As a result there was no moral self-confrontation. But for the tax collector and prostitute, who were all too aware of their shadowy side, there was always the possibility for self-confrontation, and so for a truly moral consciousness.

This is abundantly clear in the famous Parable of the Prodigal Son (Luke 15:11–32). Although the kingdom is not specifically mentioned in this parable, it is clearly a parable of the kingdom and a cornerstone of Jesus' attitude. The paradox of the parable is that the two brothers are two sides of one whole person. Each of us has a Pharasaic elder-brother side and a wayward prodigal-son side. Only when we recognize the latter can we hope to come to ourselves as the prodigal son did (Luke 15:17 KJV) and, having faced our shadowy nature, achieve the kind of higher moral consciousness the kingdom requires. Naturally this will necessitate giving up some of the moral self-esteem in which the elder brother revels.

It is this self-confrontation which leads to *commitment to the inner way* of the kingdom, and to the realization that the kingdom of God is a process, a journey, a work of life. Those who would achieve the kingdom must be resolutely committed to the inner way. If they look back yearningly to the less conscious life they enjoyed before they set out in search of the kingdom, they are not worthy of it.

'Once the hand is laid on the plough, no one who looks back is fit for the kingdom of God' (Luke 9:62).

In my counseling work I have often had occasion to reflect upon this saying of Jesus. Some persons come to the hard work of self-confrontation only under painful duress. Once a measure of their pain is alleviated, they drop the plow and turn back to the unconscious condition in which they reveled before. They are not yet ready for the kingdom.

In contrast are those who find themselves unable to leave the inner way. They are drawn to the creative process going on within them as though by a great force and nothing could bring them to leave it. Sometimes, when the going is especially painful or difficult and they complain of its demanding nature, I ask, "Could you stop this inner work if you wanted to?" The answer is, "No, I have no choice but to continue in this way." For these the kingdom of God is close at hand, and there is no longer any question of dropping the plow and turning back.

The *personal, psychological aspect* of the kingdom of God is clearly emphasized by Jesus in his repeated insistence that the new life required by the kingdom is so radical that it amounts to a complete change and renewal of personality. So Jesus says to the Pharisee Nicodemus,

'I tell you most solemnly, unless a man is born from above, he cannot see the kingdom of God' (John 3:3).

The Greek word rendered here in the Jerusalem translation "above" can also mean "again." Both meanings apply to Jesus' view of the kingdom. The individual *is* born again, an image indicating the death of an old personality and the birth of a new. This new birth is "from above"; that is, it involves the establishment in us of a higher moral and psychological consciousness. Again he states,

'I tell you solemnly, unless you change and become like little children you will never enter the kingdom of heaven. And so, the one who makes himself as little as this little child is the greatest in the kingdom of heaven' (Matthew 18:3–4/ Mark 9:35–37/Luke 9:47–48; cf. Matthew 19:14).

As we shall see later, the image of the child is used by Jesus to represent our transformed personalities because of the freedom of the child from any false, masklike front, enabling him to remain spontaneous and creative. Until adults teach them differently, children reflect on the outside what they feel on the inside; there is as yet no split between appearance and reality. So the child remains in creative contact with his inner world; the ego and the unconscious are not split apart, but have a natural and flowing relationship with each other. This is the relationship which members of the kingdom are to establish with their inner potentialities.

Naturally this involves *a realization of inner values,* and outer values take secondary consideration for those who belong to the kingdom of God. Even if outside fortune becomes adverse, there is a blessing if this is a consequence of following inner values.

'Happy those who are persecuted in the cause of right: theirs is the kingdom of heaven' (Matthew 5:10).

Money is seen as a special danger because it so easily seduces a man away from inner values into a false feeling of his power and importance:

'it is easier for a camel to pass through the eye of a needle than for a rich man to enter the kingdom of heaven' (Matthew 19:24/Luke 18:25/Mark 10:25).

To properly appreciate this saying, we must remember how shocking it was to the disciples, who declared in astonishment,

'Who can be saved, then?'

Here we see again how much Jesus had broken away from the historically conditioned attitudes of his time, for the prevailing Jewish idea was that good health and good fortune were a sign of God's favor to the deserving. This is how they got around the problem of evil, for it meant that the poor and suffering were only having divinely ordained punishment for their sin. No doubt this justified in the minds of the people of his day a great deal of social abuse, even as today some people of wealth and means look upon their material gains as their "just due."

Jesus' point is that the man with wealth is easily taken away from the search for inner values. He can identify with the worldly sense of importance which wealth brings him. power, influence, an impressive public image, a sense of his righteousness. As we will see in Chapter Five, all of this tragically takes him away from the person he is. This does not mean that it is impossible for a wealthy man to enter into the kingdom; Jesus himself adds a little later "for God everything is possible." But we might say that a man with worldly power needs to be twice as conscious as a man less subject to such seductions.

The *spiritual nature* of the kingdom of God is seen reflected in the role of the kingdom of God as the foe of evil. Just as there is a kingdom of God, so there is a kingdom of evil.

This is why works of healing are so important in the New Testament. Physical or mental illness was regarded by Jesus as an alienation from God, an evil condition to be overcome. It was inevitable that wherever the kingdom was preached, and the faith of the people permitted, works of healing would be wrought. Jesus' usual formula after healing a person was the statement, "Your faith has made you whole." This wholeness is of the essence of the kingdom; and where the kingdom is manifested in a man, wholeness is established and sickness banished. So inevitably the kingdom and healing go together, and we read of Jesus that he goes about the countryside

> Proclaiming the Good News of the kingdom and curing all kinds of diseases and sickness among the people (Matthew 4:23, 9:35).

Illness and possession were effects of the kingdom of Satan. Like the kingdom of God, the kingdom of Satan was also a spiritual reality personally manifested in men. This is clear from the story of the encounter between Jesus and the Pharisees after Jesus has healed some demoniacs. The Pharisees, jealous of Jesus' power and growing influence, accuse him of casting out devils by means of the power of Beelzebub (Satan). Jesus makes it clear that it is by God's power that he casts out demons, and that this healing is a sign that the kingdom of God is now with men.

'But if it is through the Spirit of God that I cast devils out, then know that the kingdom of God has overtaken you' (Matthew 12:28/Luke 11:20).

This kingdom of God is contrasted with the kingdom of Satan,

'Now if Satan casts out Satan, he is divided against himself; so how can his kingdom stand?' (Matthew 12:26).

Clearly the kingdom of Satan is a present spiritual reality manifested in the illnesses and possessions which Jesus healed. Similarly, the kingdom of heaven is a present, spiritual reality.

The kingdom of Satan, moreover, is *not* divided against itself. Later we will look more closely at the origin and nature of evil in Jesus' thought. Now it is enough to note that there is no question in Jesus' mind that the kingdom of Satan is *not* divided against itself. Evil is single in its intention, and this intention is to destroy wholeness. Evil is antiwholeness, and so is opposed to God's kingdom. As long as men are inwardly in conflict, divided within themselves, victims of their own inner opposition, they are easy prey for evil. But where the kingdom of God is being established in an individual, he is also becoming whole and the kingdom of evil has no power over him.

This is why the kingdom of heaven is the *supreme value of life*. Once a person has seen the treasure of the kingdom of heaven, he will be willing to pay the price, for its value is above all other values; and once a person enters into the new life of the kingdom, his relationship to the material side of life is also in order. So Jesus declares,

'Set your hearts on his kingdom first, and on his righteousness, and all these other things will be given you as well'
(Matthew 6:33/Luke 12:31).

Not even the joys of family life can compare in value to the
kingdom:

'there is no one who has left house, wife, brothers, parents or
children for the sake of the kingdom of God who will not
be given repayment many times over in this present time
and, in the world to come, eternal life' (Luke 18:29–
30/Matthew 19:29/Mark 10:29–30).

This leads us to the final paradox of the kingdom we will
present in this chapter. The kingdom of God is a present
reality, experienceable by the individual in this life, and, as
we have seen, a psychological experience requiring of the
individual a new moral consciousness, a commitment to an
inner way, self-confrontation, and a giving of priority to
inner values versus outer values. The kingdom brings to the
individual his own wholeness, meaning, and creativity, so
that the rewards of the kingdom are felt in this life.

But at the same time there is always a transcendent aspect
to the kingdom, expressed in the above sayings in which
Jesus hints at repayment to come in eternal life. Or, in
psychological terms, the individual who seeks to establish
wholeness in his life comes to belong to Life. Having
served the purposes of life in his earthly lifetime, he continues to serve a spiritual life in a world to come. Exactly
what life after death consists of we cannot know in this
earthly existence. But if life has a meaning, so does death;
and if we become whole, something indestructible is forged

in us which, in ways which pass our understanding, joins us to the fabric of eternal life. This is the ultimate promise of the kingdom of God.

The kingdom of God is a spiritual reality, personally experienced by the individual, capable of psychological description. Now it remains to discuss in more detail what entering into the kingdom means and what are the benefits of its creative new power.

PART TWO

THE INNER MEANING OF JESUS' SAYINGS

3

Entering

into the

Kingdom

✠✠✠

We have already seen
that the kingdom is within all men. But paradoxically *only
a few among the multitude will find their way to the
kingdom.* The many will pass by and not notice its reality,
and even some who have been expressly invited to enter
will not accept God's invitation. So Jesus declares,

> 'For many are called, but few are chosen' (Matthew
> 22:14).

Those who do enter the kingdom are those who have
come to recognize the reality of the inner world and to
respond to its demands upon them for consciousness. This
must always be an individual act of recognition; it cannot
be accomplished so long as we are identified with a group.
Most of us will find our sense of identity in our member-
ship in the Church, the D.A.R., the "Fatherland," the polit-
ical party, or the gang on the street corner.

One alarming thing about the current social conflict of

our times is that, whether we look to the right or the left, we see so little individuality and so much collective thinking. Man's collective nature—his deeply ingrained instinct toward herd psychology—keeps most people outside of the kingdom. Men hate and fear individuality with its demands for freedom and consciousness, and so they reject the kingdom of God. In so doing, they reject the inner world, for the recognition of a world within man destroys that identification with the group which shields us from the demands of becoming an individual.

In contrast, entrance into the kingdom requires the disidentification with the group and the assumption of the burden of being a person. This is often painful when we can no longer identify with outer collectives. Often our dreams reflect the pain of finding ourselves no longer identical with our fellows around us. In such a dream we may have just found something unusual, or have taken a little-traveled turn in a path or road. The dreamer is very much surprised and filled with a sense of wonder at the new turn of events. But there are many other people around who pass by and take no notice. The dreamer is surprised that no one else seems to feel his discovery is important, or to recognize what the dreamer himself feels is so unusual. . . . Inner reality is discovered, and already he is no longer identical with the collective spirit; to his surprise he finds that he is different. A process of the differentiation of personality has begun.

Because those who enter the kingdom must enter as individuals, the way to the kingdom is never the path of least resistance, but is a narrow, difficult, and winding way which requires us to "go against nature." As long as man is identical with a group consciousness, he follows the easiest road, inclining himself to those instincts, attitudes, and mass movements which are the easiest way to follow at the time. When any individual sets himself against the group consciousness, he begins to swim up the stream instead of down. He suffers the pain and difficulty of becoming a conscious person, no longer able to hide from his anxiety in a mass identity.

Anxiety is inevitable for those who enter into the kingdom. There is, of course, such a thing as sick anxiety, the sign of a pathologically disturbed personality. But there is also divine anxiety, the anxiety which is inevitable because entering the kingdom calls for the individual to differentiate himself from the group, accepting the consequences and responsibilities of choice. All of this is stated by Jesus in his saying in the Sermon on the Mount,

'Enter by the narrow gate, since the road that leads to perdition is wide and spacious, and many take it; but it is a narrow gate and a hard road that leads to life, and only a few find it' (Matthew 7:13–14/Luke 13:24).

The wide road is the way through life which we travel unconsciously, the road of least resistance and mass identity. The narrow road requires consciousness, close attention, lest we wander off the path. Only the few take it because of its individual character and because it entails the hardship of becoming conscious. The narrowness of the gate suggests the anxiety of this part of the process of finding the kingdom, for narrowness and anxiety have long been associated together.

Our dreams reflect this in showing us sometimes on a narrow way. In a typical dream of this kind the dreamer may be traveling down a freeway, and then turn off onto a lesser known road. Or the dreamer may find himself anxiously ascending a steep and winding path up a mountain. Or there may be a narrow way, an aperture or tunnel, through which the dreamer must fearfully pass. In both Jesus' saying and the images of our dreams, the same motif is struck: the peculiarly conscious, and therefore anxious, Way required of those who would enter the kingdom.

Those who are called upon to enter the kingdom of God may not always recognize what is happening to them. At first the approach of the kingdom may seem like a violent attack from something dark and dreadful; for when the kingdom descends upon us, the first experience is often a darkening of our old state of mind in order that a new consciousness may emerge. Psychologically this is a necessity. Entrance into the kingdom means the destruction of the old personality with its constricted and uncreative attitudes. If the kingdom is to come, this old person must die. The fortress behind which the ego has been hiding must be torn down, and as these defenses are battered down forcibly by the movement from within, it may seem at first like a violent assault. Whenever this upheaval in personality occurs, it is important that its religious overtones be realized; for if this dynamic inner process is viewed only clinically, its spiritual significance will be lost and the kingdom will not be revealed.

The violent nature of the entrance into the kingdom is reflected in many of Jesus' sayings, and is the proper explanation for Jesus' seemingly enigmatic remark:

'Up to the time of John it was the Law and the Prophets; since then, the kingdom of God has been preached, and by violence everyone is getting in' (Luke 16:16/Matthew 11:12)

as well as in the familiar saying:

'anyone who loses his life for my sake will find it' (Matthew 10:39).

The Law was a protection against a direct experience of the kingdom of God. By fulfilling the Law, men hoped to achieve their proper relationship with God without having to relate to the inner world. But it was, as Nicholas Berdyaev has said, an ethic of obedience, not of creativity.* The kingdom, however, is dynamically creative, and the ethic of the kingdom is a creative ethic based on consciousness and love, not on legalism. Now that the kingdom has come upon men, the old rigid outlook embodied in the Law will be violently assaulted so that the new and creative person may appear.

So it was with Marian. A sincerely religious woman, her religious orientation had for years been formal and external, amounting to an ethic of obedience to moral requirements and identification with the prevailing collective attitudes of her Church, so that her own creative personality was lost. This identification also served as a protection against her having to face many painful feelings that grew out of past disappointments in life and love. The result was an outwardly pleasing personality, but a separation from her own creativity as well as from her own pain. Finally

* Nicholas Berdyaev, *The Meaning of the Creative Act.*

the dam broke and the repressed unconscious elements succeeded in disorienting her outer life completely.

In the beginning of this experience she had a dream in
which she was on a ship in a violent storm, hanging onto a
slim pole which was part of the ship's superstructure. Then
she lost her grip and fell tumbling into the turbulent sea.
. . . Here was her dilemma: she had "lost her grip"—i.e.
her conscious hold on things—and had fallen into the violently disturbed waters of the unconscious. Here she would
either have to drown or learn to swim in these waters of
conflict and creativity.

In the ensuing breakdown of her life, with its anxiety
and dark depression, there was danger that the creative
possibilities in the situation might be lost. Viewed only
from a clinical perspective, the picture was bleak. Fortunately, she was able to see the meaning of her experience
and perceive that it was precisely in her darkness and
confusion that God was acting. She realized the truth of the
saying "a soul in trouble is near unto God." * The meaning
of the events which were taking place within her became
clear and, as she grasped this thread of meaning, she was
able to see the creative elements in the midst of her violent
upheaval, and to move from sickness to health, from obedience to creativity, from formal, outward religion to a religion connected meaningfully to her own inner world.

This brings us to the next paradox of entering into the
kingdom of God: *it is those who have recognized that they*

* Gregory of Nazianzus.

have been injured or hurt in some way in life who are most apt to come into the kingdom. There is no virtue in our weakness or injury as such, especially if this leads to self-pity, which completely defeats the creative purposes of the kingdom. But unless a person has recognized his own need, even his own despair, he is not ready for the kingdom, as those who feel that they are self-sufficient, whom life has upheld in their one-sided orientation, remain caught in their egocentricity.

This is why Jesus so often associated with sinners and tax collectors and was generally unable to have a relationship with the Pharisees, for the latter, as a rule, were upheld in their egocentricity by their privileged position in society and by their conviction of their own righteousness. But the sinners and tax collectors, if they turned and confronted themselves, could be receptive to the kingdom.

This paradox of the kingdom is expressed in the Parable of the Wedding Feast, in which the kingdom of God is likened to a king who gave a wedding feast in honor of his son. First he invited those who were the most respected members of the community, but they were all too busy with other things, too engrossed in their own affairs, and did not heed the king's invitation. Finally the king became angry and declared,

> 'The wedding is ready; but as those who were invited proved to be unworthy, go to the crossroads in the town and invite everyone you can find' (Matthew 22:8–9).

In Luke's version it is stated even more forcibly:

> Then the householder, in a rage, said to his servant, 'Go out quickly into the streets and alleys of the town and bring in

here the poor, the crippled, the blind and the lame. . . . Go
to the open roads and the hedgerows and *force* people to
come in to make sure my house is full' (Luke 14:21, 23;
italics mine).

Precisely those who seem the least fit for the kingdom
are those who come to enter into it. Those who are forced
by life to concede to themselves that they are psychologically crippled, maimed, or blind can be compelled to enter
into the great feast. But those who are convinced that they
are self-sufficient do not enter because they remain caught
in their own one-sidedness.

But even then there are dangers and demands, and not
everyone called to come to the feast belongs to the kingdom; one man came without a wedding garment, and he
was cast into outer darkness. According to K. C. Pillai in
his little book *Light Through an Eastern Window*, it was
the custom in the ancient Orient for a nobleman who
invited someone to his house for a special occasion to send
with his messenger a special garment to be worn by the
guest. To wear this garment was both an honor and a badge
of protection to the person as he traveled on the way to the
court. To arrive without the garment was the height of
carelessness and rudeness. Similarly, if we arrive at the
kingdom having carelessly and rudely neglected to recognize the divine author of the feast, we are cast into outer
darkness; that is, we are banished to the realm of the unconscious.

To many people this ruthless punishment seems harsh
and cruel, but we must remember that there is no sentimen-
tality about the kingdom of God. Christianity is a very
feeling religion; it must deeply involve our emotions as well

as our intellect or it will not be real. But it is not a *sentimental* religion, and the sentimentalizing of the feeling aspect of Christianity has been one of the disasters which have overtaken the Christian spirit. In the kingdom of God we are dealing with hard spiritual facts, and there is no room for sentiment. If we jump off a cliff, we may kill ourselves or break a leg; this is a physical fact, and we have no right to expect God to interfere with our fate if we flout the physical facts of His creation. But there are also spiritual facts which are just as objective and real as are physical facts. One of these is that if we come to the kingdom of God and act unconsciously, despising the things of the inner world, we can expect to be ruthlessly treated by the unconscious, for in our refusal to become conscious we have flouted the spiritual facts of creation.

A parallel to the Parable of the Wedding Feast can be noticed in counseling. Few people come to counseling who are not driven to do so from some injury in life. Others, who can maintain the illusion of self-sufficiency, will avoid contact with the inner world. They are too content and absorbed with outer things to pay attention to inner things. But those who first come to the inner world because they are forced to do so often remain to enjoy the feast. Though they are first motivated by some injury or failure in life, they may, through their contact with the inner world, not only be healed but also find the springs of creative living.

It is because of the demanding nature of the kingdom that *our entrance into it frequently involves us in a crisis.*

As we have seen, all of the old person, all the old attitudes, are challenged by the kingdom. Our response to this challenge is quite crucial and determines whether we will go the way of creativity or the way of unconsciousness. This is the "ego crisis," a time of judgment but also of opportunity. It is in this light that the sense of urgency regarding the kingdom, of which Jesus frequently speaks, is to be understood. The time is fulfilled, and man is now to respond; the consequences of turning aside the kingdom cannot be avoided, nor can man postpone his response any longer.

The mission of the twelve is a good example of this. Here Jesus sends out his disciples to spread the word of the kingdom and empowers them with "authority over unclean spirits with power to cast them out and to cure all kinds of diseases and sickness" (Matthew 10:1/Luke 9:1/Mark 6:7). The possession of this power by the disciples shows that they had, at least in some measure, been initiated into the mysteries of the kingdom. In Matthew's Gospel this mission is initially only to the lost sheep of the house of Israel. The people of Israel, as the historic bearers of the direct relationship with God, are the first to be presented with the kingdom as an imminent, inner reality. Characteristic of the disciples' mission is the sense of urgency, for

'if anyone does not welcome you or listen to what you have to say, as you walk out of the house or town shake the dust from your feet. I tell you solemnly, on the day of Judgement it will not go as hard with the land of Sodom and Gomorrah as with that town' (Matthew 10:14–15/Luke 10:10–12).

It may be surprising that what will befall the people of Israel who deny the kingdom will be worse than the fate of Sodom and Gomorrah, for there is no reason to suppose that the people of Israel led worse lives than those Old Testament unbelievers. Again, this has to do with the matter of obedience versus creativity. The people of Sodom and Gomorrah were disobedient to God. They had turned aside God's laws and lived only for their own pleasure. The people of Israel fulfilled more completely the demands of obedience, but the kingdom's demand is not for obedience but for creativity, not for a religion of outward observances but for consciousness. The reason things will go so badly for the people of Israel who deny the kingdom is not that they are so disobedient, but that the kingdom and its call to consciousness are close at hand, and this creates a situation of crisis.

The same crisis often occurs in the development of the kingdom within an individual. At some point in our inner development, there may come a desire on our part to stop the creative inner process, to decide "This is enough; I need go no further." Often there then sets in a time of darkness and confusion worse than the first. Such an experience is a sure sign that the creative process of the kingdom *will not be denied*—that if one turns aside the demands of the creative, and seeks to return to a life of unconscious obedience, his fate will be worse than that of Sodom and Gomorrah. God can be harder on those who are close to Him than on those who have never known Him, precisely because *they* may achieve something creative.

So it was with Paula, who came to counseling because of a high degree of anxiety which interfered with her work

and paralyzed her life. After several consultations the counselor and counselee were pleased with the progress. The
anxiety seemed to have diminished, and she was functioning very well. At this point, with the blessing of the counselor, she decided to terminate therapy, only to find that
her anxiety returned and was, if anything, even greater
than before. Subsequent therapy showed that a creative
process was at work within her which could not be denied.
In her desire to return to "normalcy" and be again her "old
self," this creative process would have had to be aborted.
Had she persisted in turning aside the call to a more creative calling, her fate might have been "worse than Sodom
and Gomorrah." Fortunately, she obeyed the inner call and
her development continued. In time her anxiety disap-
peared again, but this time she did not break off her relationship with her inner world.

In this crisis of consciousness the personality must become new. The old personality simply cannot contain the
new state of consciousness which the kingdom demands
from us. If the new personality is poured into the old
framework, the old framework will burst asunder. The
creative contents of the kingdom require a new and fresh
consciousness to hold them. Many a person has sought to
cling too long to the old personality and under the impact
of the kingdom has disintegrated. For the kingdom is a
"new wine," and the new wine of consciousness demands a
new wineskin to hold it:

'No one puts a piece of unshrunken cloth on to an old cloak,
because the patch pulls away from the cloak and the tear
gets worse. Nor do people put new wine into old wineskins;

if they do, the skins burst, the wine runs out, and the skins are lost. No; they put new wine into fresh skins and both are preserved' (Matthew 9:16–17/Mark 2:21–22/Luke 5:36–39).

It is because of the crisis-bringing nature of the kingdom that it has the power to bring a storm into our lives. As in the case of Marian, who dreamed that she was thrown into the sea, the ego may be thrust into the turbulent life of the unconscious with all its conflicts and demands. When this happens, an ingredient called "faith" is of crucial importance, for with this ingredient one finds that the storm is not chaotic but is under the control of the higher power of the Son of Man. The storm is great indeed, but the Power of God is greater, and all the turbulent events are under His authority as He establishes Himself in the soul.

Our dreams are often filled with the image of the storm. We may be on a stormy ocean, or driving into a great black cloud, or shaken by an approaching earthquake, or exposed to a driving wind and rain. In this time of storm faith is essential. But this is not an intellectual faith which consists in giving assent to creedal doctrines; it is an inner attitude, a committing ourselves to the inner way regardless of what comes, a determination to know the One who is at the center of the conflict.

It is in this sense that the story of the calming of the storm is to be understood (Luke 8:22–25). This storm, which may be understood in much the same way as a dream, begins with our Lord saying to the disciples,

'Let us cross over to the other side of the lake'.

Here is the image of the sea journey, the crossing over
the waters of the unconscious to another stage on the journey. As an ancient Chinese wisdom book says, "It furthers
one to cross the great waters." Typically such a passage is a
stormy one, and in this story the storm does come and the
little boat of the disciples, their tiny ego standpoint, is
tossed to and fro on turbulent seas. Terrified, they rouse
the Master,

'Master! Master! We are going down!'

This is the deepest fear of the ego: that it will drown in
the unconscious, be overcome and extinguished. Many people become so fainthearted that they abandon the journey
entirely at this point. They turn back to safety, or drown
out of sheer fright. Only faith can give us the strength to
persevere through the difficulties of the storm.

Then he woke up and rebuked the wind and the rough
water; and they subsided and it was calm again. He said to
them, 'Where is your faith?' They were awestruck and
astonished and said to one another, 'Who can this be, that
gives orders even to winds and waves and they obey him?'

The inner world, as well as the outer world, is obedient
to God. In Christ, God is realized within man as well as in
the forces of the world outside of him. With faith in this
power of God one may endure even the storm.

But ultimately the power to withstand the storm of exposure to the inner world is the rock of consciousness of the
Word of God. The ego standpoint is often represented as a
house. If one puts one's faith in things other than conscious-

ness of the meaning of God's Word in the soul, the house of the ego cannot stand. The image of the house is an important one in Jesus' sayings, and in our dreams. In our dreams the kind of house we have typically symbolizes our conscious framework. One man dreams of living in a room with no windows and no doors. It represents a condition of his consciousness which does not have any outlook on life and which keeps him shut in.* Another person dreams of finding herself unexpectedly living in a great and beautiful house. She is thrilled and delighted. But the house has another side to it which remains unexplored and frightening to her. Her new consciousness is exciting and greatly expanded, but it also contains many new possibilities which she must now come to recognize, and which have within them an element of fear because they represent something unknown. Jesus says of the storm and the house,

> 'everyone who listens to these words of mine and acts on them will be like a sensible man who built his house on rock. Rain came down, floods rose, gales blew and hurled themselves against that house, and it did not fall: it was founded on rock' (Matthew 7:24–25/Luke 6:47–48).

Here the house stands amid the storm because it was founded upon rock. This rock is the rock of consciousness. It comes from hearing and acting upon the words of Jesus; that is, by fulfilling the demands of the ethic of consciousness and creativity. It is spiritual consciousness and insight which form the rock of Christ on which the kingdom is founded, as appears also from the often misinterpreted story of the confession of Peter on the road to Caesarea Philippi (Matthew 16:13–20).

* See Chapter I of my book *Dreams: God's Forgotten Language*.

In this story Jesus and his disciples are traveling to Caesarea Philippi when Jesus asks his disciples,

'Who do people say the Son of Man is?'

The disciples give various speculations identifying Jesus with one or another of the prophets of Israel. Jesus then counters with a direct thrust at his disciples,

'But you, who do you say I am?'

Then Simon Peter speaks up,

'You are the Christ, the Son of the living God'.

And Jesus replies,

'Simon son of Jonah, you are a happy man! Because it was not flesh and blood that revealed this to you but my Father in heaven. So I now say to you: You are Peter and on this rock I will build my Church. And the gates of the underworld can never hold out against it. I will give you the keys of the kingdom of heaven: whatever you bind on earth shall be considered bound in heaven; whatever you loose on earth shall be considered loosed in heaven.'

What Jesus congratulates Peter on is his *spiritual insight*. Peter has become *conscious*, and on this rests both his faith and his authority. In the Greek, Jesus calls Simon "Petros," the masculine for "rock," and then refers to "this petra," the feminine form of the word. Peter's authority is founded upon his "petra," the rock of his conscious insight. It is against this principle of consciousness that even the storms from the underworld, the hellish assault of the chaotic forces of the unconscious, cannot prevail.

The rock is not Peter the person, but the *insight* of Peter, the act of consciousness. Wherever this act of consciousness is made, the Church exists.

People with this insight are enormously important. Here is another paradox of the kingdom: While God is central to it, man is also indispensable, because man's consciousness is vital. For this reason *man himself is given the keys to the kingdom of God*. Man, as the bearer of consciousness, is that important in God's plan. Here Jesus goes far beyond the ethic of obedience to the ethic of creativity. Man is now much more than a fallen creature needing to be restored; he is a creative creature endowed by God with a fundamental significance in the total scheme of things.

The kingdom is now at hand. Man may enter into it, and is called to it by God. The entrance to the kingdom is often a violent one, for entering into the kingdom means surrendering the old personality and finding a new wine. This new wine of a consciously lived life requires the new person. The new life is to be founded on the ethic of creative consciousness, and such a life is tremendously important to God Himself. The kingdom is at hand. We have seen its meaning, and we wish to enter it; we are ready to become disciples. But what will be demanded of us as disciples of the kingdom of God? It is to this that we now turn.

4

The
Price of
Discipleship

✤✤✤

By instinct man is a group animal. For hundreds of thousands of years he has existed through the group, and the individual has found his identity and meaning by virtue of his inclusion in tribe, clan, or nation. But the kingdom of God calls us to go beyond this ancient herd instinct and to establish an individual consciousness of oneself and of God. Being a disciple means following the call to the individual Way, and inevitably this will mean the separating out of oneself from the collective psychology of the group.

This tendency to submerge ourselves in the group is a principal source of our remaining unconscious and may exist with our Church, our family, our nation, our business, a branch of the armed services, whatever it is with which we identify and in terms of which we define ourselves. Separating ourselves from the group identification is a painful process, for as long as we remain submerged in the group, we find a certain security. When this unconscious identification gives way, as it must under the impact of the kingdom of God, the illusory peace is shattered.

So Jesus declares,

'Do not suppose that I have come to bring peace to the earth: it is not peace I have come to bring, but a sword' (Matthew 10:34/Luke 12:51).

A sword is that which divides and separates. Christ as the Word of God is a living sword, dividing and separating what was once merged together in order that individual differentiation may take place.

This process of becoming an individual may also be likened to a purging process in which the individual, no longer secure in group identification, finds himself plunged into the inner fire, there to be purged, purified, and made fit for the kingdom. In the group we are protected from direct contact with the fiery nature of the process of coming into selfhood, but when we stand alone we feel the burning intensity of the inner life.

'I have come to bring fire to the earth, and how I wish it were blazing already!' (Luke 12:49).

It is interesting to compare this verse with a similar one from the apocryphal Gospel According to Thomas,

Whoever is near to me is near to the fire, and whoever is far from me is far from the Kingdom (Logion 82).

A part of the process of becoming an individual necessarily involves a psychological separation from family identifi-

cation. To find ourselves, we must be free from unconscious identification with parents, wife or husband, and
children. We cannot fulfill the demands of discipleship for
individuality so long as we are identified with what Fritz
Kunkel has called "tribal consciousness." * It makes no
difference whether this is an outer identification with
mother, father, husband, or wife, which keeps us from
becoming ourselves because we are living through someone
else, or whether it is an inner identification, and we carry
father, mother, husband, or wife on the inside as an inner
voice, a dominating spirit. The only way to achieve this
break from tribal loyalties, which are among the strongest
earthly loyalties man has, is to ground one's life on the still
higher loyalty demanded from those who would become
disciples of the kingdom. This sacrifice of the old loyalties
often seems incredibly hard, even cruel, so Jesus says,

> 'For I have come to set a man against his father, a daughter
> against her mother, a daughter-in-law against her mother-
> in-law. A man's enemies will be those of his own household'
> (Matthew 10:35–36).

It may seem strange that Jesus should point to the members of one's own family as "enemies." It is precisely because there is so much love, and so much tribal loyalty, that
one's own family can be an "enemy" to the kingdom of
God. There is no difficulty in denying what we dislike for
the sake of the kingdom of God, but to deny what seems
closest to us, what seems to be the supreme loyalty in life, is
extremely difficult. This is what makes it necessary for the

* In *Creation Continues.*

disciple of the kingdom to see what an "enemy" these close ties are.

It is in this sense that we must understand Jesus' seemingly harsh words regarding the necessity to renounce all that we hold most dear to us:

> Great crowds accompanied him on his way and he turned and spoke to them. 'If any man comes to me without hating his father, mother, wife, children, brothers, sisters, yes and his own life too, he cannot be my disciple' (Luke 14:25–26).

Often when an identification exists with our families which is thwarting our individuality, this motif of "hating" appears in our dreams. The dream in which we reject mother or father, or in which we fight against one whom we feel we love, often represents the need to inwardly break from an unconscious identification with a family figure. The fight, quarrel, or struggle against someone in our dream expresses the need to differentiate ourselves psychologically in order that we may become free and individual.

Our dreams here furnish us with a helpful insight into the meaning of Jesus' sayings, for they point out that it is the inward "hating" which is called for, not an outward hating. Jesus' words are no justification for quarreling with the members of one's family, no excuse for hurting them on the basis that this is finding our individuality. It is the reverse: we quarrel outwardly with those from whom we are not inwardly disidentified. It is the failure to distinguish our individuality from those to whom we are close which

forces us into broken relationships. By taking Jesus' words
inwardly, effecting an inward separation, we can avoid
being compelled to an outward separation. Becoming individual, realizing our own identity within, we can then
relate creatively and positively to our family for the first
time.

Albert finds himself in his early forties working at a job
with little prestige, scope for creativity, money, or future,
in a weakened physical and psychological condition. De-
pressed, he comes for counsel. Eventually the picture
emerges of a man who might have had a creative career but
let his career drop in favor of a secure but mediocre job
because of his feeling that the first task in life is to provide
safety and security for his family. Behind this conviction is
the personality of his mother, a manipulating person, rig-
idly conventional in her attitudes, reinforcing the power of
her opinions with various destructive ways of forcing those
close to her to follow her dictates by playing on their
emotions.

Albert has never "hated" his mother sufficiently. He
carries her within him as an inner voice, and is a slave to her
mediocrity and her uncreative standards. He never quar-
reled with her outwardly, nor did he break with her inwardly, but remained caught in an unconscious identification with her, allowing her conventional opinions to rule
him. Now, for the creativity of the kingdom to come into
his life, the son must be divided against the mother. He
must break with her inwardly and become capable of refusing to play the neurotic and manipulative games by means
of which she seeks to retain her hold on her children. He
must face the possibility of open conflict with her and must

risk himself in a creative future, rejecting the mediocrity he previously accepted because he had set his loyalty to and fascination for mother above the commitment to the kingdom of God.

John and Mary are a happily married young couple. Each sees in the other the fulfillment he or she is seeking. They are in love and look forward to a life together in which each person supplies perfectly the needs of the other. But strangely, idyllic though the situation seems, quarrels begin to come. They are surprisingly bitter, and neither one can understand why the other is disappointing them so. There is danger that their earlier love will turn to bitterness and reproach, that where before they were drawn together, now they will be driven apart. From their conscious point of view it looks only like bad faith on the part of the other person, a betrayal from the one on whom they had pinned their hopes. But from the point of view of their inner development it is different. Here is seen the picture of a man identifying his soul with the woman he loves, and a woman finding her own fulfillment in a relationship with this man. Each is fulfilled only through the other, and their individuality is aborted.

Before individuality can come there must be psychological differentiation. The unconscious identification each partner makes with the other must be broken, and each one must recognize his or her uniqueness. The divine call to seek fulfillment not through absorption in another person, but through relationship with himself, with the other, and with God, must be accepted. When a couple like John and Mary does not want this much consciousness, the unconscious draws the sword and forces on the couple what they have been too unconscious to see for themselves. So quarrels come and drive them apart. If they see the meaning underlying this phase of their relationship, they can go on to a new and more real relatedness together, each growing by understanding his and the other person's uniqueness. If they do not see, then only rejection of the other, which will also be self-rejection, can ensue.

The breaking of the tribal consciousness and establishment of an individual consciousness must not be confused with egoism. It is not a matter of living only for oneself but of being able to come into real relationships with people, since now for the first time we are real persons. The circle of our relationships now grows. We no longer confine our relatedness to those of our own circle, to our own tribal group, but can respond to all persons, of all kinds and types. It is not a matter of being insular. To the contrary, now we can leave our insularity and can understand what it means to be part of a brotherhood of man under a common heavenly Father.

This is especially important for our present social situation in America in which the ancient tribal consciousness is driving the black, brown, and white man into their separate camps. Only the man who is becoming his individual self can accept others outside his tribal group as his brothers. Those who have identified with the tribal collective will tend to see others outside his group as "enemies." This is why the following saying of Jesus is so important:

He was still speaking to the crowds when his mother and his brothers appeared; they were standing outside and were anxious to have a word with him. But to the man who told him this Jesus replied, 'Who is my mother? Who are my brothers?' And stretching out his hand towards his disciples he said, 'Here are my mother and my brothers. Anyone who does the will of my Father in heaven, he is my brother and sister and mother' (Matthew 12:46–50/Luke 8:19–21/Mark 3:31–35).

Being a disciple of the kingdom means putting our loyalty to the kingdom first and sacrificing all other loyalties in life to this loyalty. But many cannot make the sacrifice that is required. They are held by sentiment rather than by feeling; they are drawn to the things of God but cannot give up their tribal values.

So a disciple of Jesus comes to him and says he would like to follow him, but adds,

'Sir, let me go and bury my father first'.

But Jesus replies,

'Follow me, and leave the dead to bury their dead' (Matthew 8:22/Luke 9:59–60).

We must recall the great filial loyalty which existed in those times toward one's parents. The desire of the would-be disciple to wait until he had buried his father does not necessarily mean that his father is now dead and that it is only a matter of delaying a few days for the proper funeral. It is more likely that it was a matter of this man's wanting to remain at home until all proper filial responsibilities toward an aging father had been fulfilled. Then he would come and follow Jesus. But Jesus' remark makes it clear that not even what was then supposed to be a supreme and divinely ordained loyalty to one's father should come between a man and the call to the kingdom. If the kingdom of God called this man to become a follower of Jesus, all other loyalties must be sacrificed. So the call to the kingdom must come before our loyalty to family, to Church, to our country. No other commitment can be allowed to come before our commitment to the following of the inner way.

This separation from an unconscious identification with persons or groups often incurs a painful sense of aloneness and disorientation. No longer is it possible to identify ourselves in terms of external factors. We are no longer this or that, members of a particular Church, employed in a certain position in the world, or related to certain people. Now we must face ourselves nakedly. This is often reflected in dreams in which we walk alone up a long road, or are trekking over a desert, or are sailing on the sea in a small boat, or are watching others pass by to whom we do not belong. Or there may be a scene in which all the others are dressed in some uniform but we are "out of step," conspicuous by some odd piece of attire. This isolation means the beginning of relationships with people, not the end of them. But the relationships in the future will have to be real relationships, not relationships founded on mutual identification or the wearing of a mask. And since there are relatively few persons ready to enter into a genuine person-to-person relationship, the first state of the discovery of our individuality can be a lonely one. So we read in Matthew,

One of the scribes then came up and said to him, 'Master, I will follow you wherever you go'. Jesus replied, 'Foxes have holes and the birds of the air have nests, but the Son of Man has nowhere to lay his head' (Matthew 8:19–20/Luke 9:57–58).

This is the image of the spiritual wanderer, one who has nowhere "to lay his head," no earthly reference point to which he can turn for his identity. But such a person can now experience himself as a son of God. No longer being identified with the collective world, he can for the first time know what the sonship of God means.

In John's Gospel the Pharisees are horrified that Jesus calls himself "Son of God." But Jesus points out to them,

'Is it not written in your Law:
I said, you are gods?
So the Law uses the word gods
of those to whom the word of God was addressed'
(John 10:34)

Blasphemous as it may sound, we are intended to be sons of God. Psychologically this becomes possible when consciousness is no longer contained in the collective but is in direct communion with the archetypal, life-giving, and numinous contents of the inner world. One then experiences the inner world as the fire, the great wind, or the intense light, symbols which frequently appear in dreams which coincide with a time in our development when such sonship is possible.

The demands of the kingdom for perseverance, for choice and commitment, and for separation from group

identification are certainly great, but the rewards are great also. Becoming an individual is painful, but it brings the treasure. Being directly in contact with the inner world and in person-to-person relationship with others, we now realize the spiritual heritage of those who enter the kingdom. With this comes the stunning realization of the unique value which our life holds in God's eyes.

Christianity is the religion of individuality. It is the great affirmation of man, who has his high calling in the universe directly from God. It is individual man who is capable of communion with God, and whose personality is eternally sanctified by having been visited by God Himself in Christ. In Christianity God is not remote and unconcerned about man. Incredibly, God yearns to restore man to his wholeness and is keenly aware of each individual.

'Can you not buy two sparrows for a penny? And yet not one falls to the ground without your Father knowing. Why, every hair on your head has been counted. So there is no need to be afraid; you are worth more than hundreds of sparrows' (Matthew 10:29–31).

The value of individuality is a striking feature of our inner life. It is revealed in the analysis of dreams, in which it becomes apparent that there is a creative power in us working intelligently to bring about our uniqueness. This is why in my previous book I called dreams "God's Forgotten Language." This is an aspect of Christianity too long overlooked. In dwelling exclusively on man's fall, on the need for man to be obedient to God and be restored from his fallen state to a sort of blamelessness, traditional theology has missed the significance of the kingdom of God. For the kingdom is not obedience, but creativity; it is not restoration to a former primitive state from which man fell, but is reunification on a much higher level.

This high calling may even seem terrible or dreadful, as it did to a woman who dreamed that she saw a beautiful rose on a table in a room and wondered to whom it belonged. When the realization came to her, "It is for you," this seemed like a terrible, blasphemous thing, and she awoke in terror. The rose represented the fulfillment, the wholeness intended uniquely for her. It seemed blasphemous that such a unique and beautiful thing was to be presented to her guilt-ridden soul. Yet Jesus boldly declares,

'So if anyone declares himself for me in the presence of men, I will declare myself for him in the presence of my Father in heaven' (Matthew 10:32).

Here it is more than a matter of witnessing for Christ in the human community. In declaring himself for Christ, a person affirms his whole life as God-given and uniquely creative. Such an individual life brings the highest value and is felt even "in heaven"; that is, it affects the course of spiritual evolution.

The Old Testament stressed the importance to God of the nation of Israel. Oriental religions stressed that man might, through the inner life of meditation and renunciation of the world, merge back into the divinity. But Jesus declared that God specifically created the individual, sought for the fulfillment of the individual, and longed to

relate to the individual. For Jesus there is no merging of the
personality back into the divine, but the affirmation of
personality in all its completeness. For this reason, while
there is mysticism in Christianity, and there is the unitive
vision, it is not primarily a mystical religion but a psychological religion. Not absorption into God, but personality
fulfillment and relationship to God, are the goals of Christianity. *This is a goal open to all men in a way that*

The unique appreciation of the value of the individual
life shows very clearly, for instance, in Jesus' words to the
Pharisees regarding man and the Sabbath. Time and again
Jesus offends the Pharisees by performing an act of healing
on the Sabbath. This was breaking the religious law; it was
offending the Sabbath rule, supposed to be the highest
demand God made upon man. But Jesus makes it clear that
people are more important to the Father than rules, that the
best of religious rules and institutions exist for the benefit of
man, not the other way around. So when challenged by the
Pharisees after healing a man with a withered hand on the
Sabbath Day he declares,

> 'If any one of you here had only one sheep and it fell down
> a hole on the sabbath day, would he not get hold of it and
> lift it out? Now a man is far more important than a sheep, so
> it follows that it is permitted to do good on the sabbath day'
> (Matthew 12:11–12/Luke 6:9–10/Mark 3:4).

The point here is not only that man is more important than
a sheep, but that each man is only *one of a kind*. For he
says,

> 'If any one of you here had only *one* sheep . . .'

God has only *one* of each individual human being, and this is more important to Him than anything else. So for this reason Jesus can also declare,

> 'The sabbath was made for man, not man for the sabbath; so the Son of Man is master even of the sabbath' (Mark 2:27–28/Matthew 12:8/Luke 6:5).

So we have the paradox of discipleship. Being a disciple for the sake of the kingdom of God looks very difficult. It makes demands upon us for choices and for ultimate commitment. It allows us to place no other values in life higher than the calling to consciousness. The call to discipleship brings a sword, it divides us from others, it forces us onto an anxious way, it comes like a fire. But at the same time, because the way of the kingdom is the way of fulfillment, it is also the easy way; and the demands Christ lays upon us, once we have assumed them, prove light. For it is always better to become conscious than to remain caught in unconsciousness, to voluntarily accept the demands the kingdom lays upon its disciples rather than experience the kingdom negatively as an adverse power in our lives. For those who deny the kingdom, who turn aside from the path of consciousness, do not escape from the demands of the kingdom. They are experienced only negatively in one's life, and what could have been fulfillment becomes destruction. So Jesus says of those who become disciples of the Way,

> 'Shoulder my yoke and learn from me, for I am gentle and humble in heart, and you will find rest for your souls. Yes,

my yoke is easy and my burden light' (Matthew
11:29–30).

Understanding this paradox is easier when we relate Jesus' image to our knowledge of the unconscious. The unconscious is like a great weight when it affects us in a way
we do not understand. The one who has no relationship to
his unconscious world is affected by it but experiences it
negatively as a dark burden. This heaviness of the unreal-
ized inner world is suggested in dreams by the familiar motif of trying to run but finding it impossible or extremely
difficult to move, as though affected by extreme inertia. On
the other hand, when the inner world is consciously experienced, it can give to consciousness a first experience of
freedom. To know the inner realm is to be free from its
heaviness and to experience its creativity. In this creativity
lies our freedom. What once burdened us now gives us
strength; we may now in our dreams make even a steep
ascent with agility.

The yoke of Christ is the yoke of becoming conscious.
This yoke is a burden, and, as we have seen, it lays require-
ments on us; but in the long run it is a light burden, and the
One whom we now serve is gentle and humble in heart.
We find that in the service of this One there is "perfect
freedom." *

---

* ". . . in knowledge of whom standeth our eternal life, whose service
is perfect freedom" (A Collect for Peace, Book of Common Prayer).

5

The
Pharisee
in Each
of Us

✠✠✠

One reason that the requirements of the kingdom are both difficult and light is the necessity to shed the Pharasaic outer mask. The mask is the person we pretend to be—the false outer personality which we turn to the world, but which is contradicted from within. The mask is that which conceals our real thoughts and feelings, and which we come to use so habitually as a way to hide from others and ourselves that we become unaware we have assumed it.

There is a certain usefulness to this outer mask, for to some extent we need it to function in the world. The destructive aspect of the mask is our tendency to identify with it, to think that we *are* the person we pretend to be, and thereby to remain unconscious of our real self. Because we identify with our outer shell and overlook the feelings and thoughts that lie within, there arises a gulf between the appearance and the reality. We no longer *are* the person we *seem* to be, so that a certain falseness has taken us over.

This brings a diminution of our creativity. By assuming for ourselves a false outer personality, we fall into a paralyzing inner contradiction which takes a great deal of our energy to maintain. Like a nation whose main energies may be absorbed in manning garrisons against an enemy, so our main energies are now taken up with maintaining our front and holding back the forces in ourselves which would contradict and overwhelm it, and the result is spiritual and psychological stagnation.

If we would belong to the kingdom, this false outer front must go. We must cease to identify with an outer mask, and the gulf between the *seem* and the *is* must shrink. We must dare to be ourselves, and must no longer hide behind a façade. Only in this way can the falseness of our personalities be overcome and a genuine self, fit for the kingdom, appear.

This shedding of the mask is the primary point of Jesus' teachings against Pharisaism. Jesus is opposed to the Pharisees primarily because the Pharisees wear masks—they conceal themselves—and so mislead men because they themselves are false. To make his point, Jesus uses a choice word to apply to the Pharisees, "hypocrites." Alluding to the Pharisees, he says,

'So when you give alms, do not have it trumpeted before you; this is what the hypocrites do in the synagogues and in the streets to win men's admiration' (Matthew 6:2).

Elsewhere he rebukes the Pharisees who criticized him for healing a crippled woman on the sabbath day:

'Hypocrites! Is there one of you who does not untie his ox or his donkey from the manger on the sabbath and take it out for watering? And this woman, a daughter of Abraham whom Satan has held bound these eighteen years—was it not right to untie her bonds on the sabbath day?' (Luke 13:15–16).

The word "hypocrite" means an "actor," and an actor in Jesus' time literally wore a mask which depicted the role he was playing. So the hypocrite was the mask-wearer, the one who was not real but was acting a role in life. In the saying about alms the role that the hypocrites wish to play is that of the important, benevolent person. They wish to win the admiration of men that they may be puffed up and think highly of themselves. In the role of philanthropic and generous men they seem to have a desire to help others. But in their hearts the motive is self-interest and the desire to make a good appearance. So the outer and the inner contradict each other, and the appearance and the reality disagree.

More than anything else, it was Jesus' seeing through this front which angered the Pharisees and made most of them his enemies. In this respect Jesus shows himself much more concerned with sins of the spirit than with sins of the flesh. In terms of the sins of the flesh the Pharisees were virtuous people. But wearing a mask is a sin of the spirit, which is much more dangerous than a sin of the flesh because it strikes at the vitals of the soul. So Jesus in his famous seven woes strikes right at the heart of the Pharisees' spiritual sickness. Like a surgeon he lays bare what is in their hearts:

'Alas for you, scribes and Pharisees, you hypocrites! You who clean the outside of cup and dish and leave the inside full of extortion and intemperance. . . . You who are like whitewashed tombs that look handsome on the outside, but

inside are full of dead men's bones and every kind of
corruption. . . .' (Matthew 23:25, 27/Luke 11:39–40).

To grasp the force of these sayings of Jesus regarding the
Pharisees, we must remember that in the popular view these
men were the most perfect examples possible of what God
wanted a man to be like. These were *the* respectable, virtuous persons in society, and now Jesus was likening them
to tombs of corruption and cups of filth! In so doing, he
was shocking the multitude. But worse yet, he was also
stripping away from the Pharisees their masks and exposing
them to themselves. For this he was never forgiven, for
there is no hatred more bitter than hatred for one who
strips away from us the façade behind which we have been
hiding.

Yet this task has to be done, for in the ethic of the
kingdom of God falseness cannot be accepted. Only a
genuine personality, no matter how sinful or dubious his
life may be, can enter into the kingdom. The kingdom
requires a depth-morality which penetrates through the
outer shell of a man to his heart. So Jesus says to the
astonished multitude in the Sermon on the Mount,

> 'if your virtue goes no deeper than that of the scribes and
> Pharisees, you will never get into the kingdom of heaven'
> (Matthew 5:20).

I say "astonished" quite deliberately. The idea that one's
morality must go deeper than that of the scribes and Pharisees, who seemed the paragons of virtue, must have been
deeply puzzling and disturbing to those who heard Jesus'
words. But Jesus can say this with authority, for he knows

that a man is made up of an inner self as well as the outer
front, and that only an *ethic which reaches to what is
within—that is, only an ethic of consciousness—is a fit
ethic for the kingdom.*

A man may try to pass himself off as someone he is not,
relying upon his outer mask to do the deception, but there
remains the unconscious, "the heart" or inner man, and this
is unaffected by the outer lie. So Jesus says to the Pharisees,

> 'You are the very ones who pass yourselves off as virtuous in
> people's sight, but God knows your hearts. For what is
> thought highly of by men is loathsome in the sight of God'
> (Luke 16:15).

This "heart" of man is a synonym for the unconscious. It
is the inner world of man where there are thoughts and
feelings and images which, though not conscious to him,
nevertheless profoundly affect him and make up his true
nature. The man who takes his "heart" seriously ultimately
arrives at the kingdom, for it is when we consciously accept
the inner world that the possibility for wholeness emerges.
As mentioned in the introduction, it is this realm of the
heart of which the prophet Daniel spoke when he told
King Nebuchadnezzar that his dream had come to him

> 'for this sole purpose: that the king should learn what it
> means, and that you should understand your inmost
> thoughts' (Daniel 2:30).

It is because of the reality of the heart of man that the
Pharasaic attitude is so destructive to the one who would
enter the kingdom. *Man's greatest delusion is thinking that*

he can avoid the unconscious and solve the moral problems
of life by creating a righteous exterior, or by an ethic of
outer obedience to laws. But this is of no avail, for God sees
into the heart of man; ruthlessly His eye penetrates into the
deepest recess of the soul. The Psalmist cried,

> 'Yahweh, you examine me and know me,
> . . . .
> you read my thoughts from far away,
> . . . .
>
> The word is not even on my tongue,
>
> Yahweh, before you know all about it;
> . . . .
> Where could I go to escape your spirit?
> Where could I flee from your presence?'
> (Psalm 139:1, 2, 4, 7)

The God whom Jesus proclaims is the God

> 'unto whom all hearts are open, all desires known, and from
> whom no secrets are hid' (The Collect, Book of Common
> Prayer, page 67).

For with God nothing can be kept in darkness, as Jesus
declares to his disciples when warning them against the
Pharisees:

> 'Be on your guard against the yeast of the Pharisees—that is,
> their hypocrisy. Everything that is now covered will be
> uncovered, and everything now hidden will be made clear.
> For this reason, whatever you have said in the dark will be

heard in the daylight, and what you have whispered in
hidden places will be proclaimed on the housetops' (Luke
12:1–3).

For this is the God "who sees all that is done in secret"
(Matthew 6:4).

With the ripping away of the masks we have been wearing and the exposure of what has been hidden within, we
come to the key to the ethic of the kingdom. *The ethic of
the kingdom is a radically new ethic because it is based on
the inner man and takes into account what is in the "heart"
of man. It is founded upon the way of consciousness, for
only the man who is conscious of his total self, and whose
"heart" is not hidden to him, can reach a deeper morality
than that of the scribes and Pharisees.* All else is a façade
and bars the way to the kingdom.

Like all of Jesus' insights, his insight into the Pharasaic
mask has implications for the social scene as well as for the
individual's own development. What we seem to be witnessing today is an awareness on the part of a whole generation that many of the values of the previous generation
have been hypocritical. Young people often point out that
while the "fathers" of our time are quick to condemn
violence on the part of various groups seeking to gain their
end, they endorse violence as a matter of national policy
against nonwhite races overseas. It seems a glaring inconsis-
tency to many young people that the use of certain relatively innocuous drugs is a felony, yet drunk drivers are
allowed to go virtually unpunished and death-dealing ciga-
rettes are promoted with multimillion dollar advertising
programs. And they are quick to perceive that the demo-

cratic ideals officially espoused and adulated are often applied with vast amounts of discrimination.

The result is an angry generation which wants to tear off the mask and "tell it like it is." On the other hand, the younger generation is as oblivious of its own failings as it is aware of the failings of its elders. So the result is not salvation but a polarization in the social order of forces which exist within the unconscious of each individual. An older generation tending to an unconscious Pharasaism clings to its concepts of order, confronted by a Dionysian younger generation intent upon tearing off the mask but sometimes having only chaos, not reform, to offer. Though this is, of course, a generalization of a complex social scene, it illustrates the way in which the conflicts within the individual become concretized in the social sphere.

Now we are in a position to see why the pursuit of wealth and worldly power is so dangerous to a man's relationship with the kingdom. Partly this is a result of the conflict between commitment to worldly gains and commitment to spiritual goals:

'No servant can be the slave of two masters: he will either hate the first and love the second, or treat the first with respect and the second with scorn. You cannot be the slave both of God and of money' (Luke 16:13).

Along the same line we have the story (Luke 18:18–23/Matthew 19:16–22/Mark 10:17–22) of the rich young man who asked Jesus,

'Good Master, what have I to do to inherit eternal life?'

Jesus urged him to follow the commandments, but the young man answered,

'I have kept all these from my earliest days till now.'

Realizing that here is a person whose soul will not be satisfied except with the highest spiritual goals—that is, with entering the kingdom of God—Jesus prescribes,

'There is still one thing you lack. Sell all that you own and distribute the money to the poor, and you will have treasure in heaven; then come, follow me.' But when he heard this he was filled with sadness, for he was very rich (Luke 18:22–23).

Here the conflict is between commitments. A man who seeks the kingdom of God cannot put worldly goals ahead of his spiritual goals. He must give to the world its due and "Render therefore unto Caesar the things which are Caesar's; and unto God the things that are God's" (Matthew 22:21 KJV). Where a conflict of commitments and loyalties occurs, the loyalty to the spiritual reality must come first. But beneath this problem of the conflict of commitments is the problem of the mask, as is clear from the conclusion of the above story.

We have already noted the following saying of Jesus in our discussion of the kingdom of God as a discovery of inner values. As we refer to it again, we can now see more distinctly just how the possession of wealth threatens our attaining the true values of the kingdom:

Jesus looked at him and said, 'How hard it is for those who
have riches to make their way into the kingdom of God!
Yes, it is easier for a camel to pass through the eye of a
needle than for a rich man to enter the kingdom of God.' 'In
that case' said the listeners 'who can be saved?' 'Things that
are impossible for men' he replied 'are possible for God.'
(Luke 18:24–27/Matthew 19:23–26/Mark 10:23–27).

Commentators often question the reference to a camel's
passing through the eye of a needle. Some suppose the "eye
of a needle" to have been a particularly narrow gate in
Jerusalem. Others conjecture that the word "camel" may,
in the original Aramaic, have been the word for "rope."
Such attempts to soften the forces of Jesus' saying are
unnecessary, for Jesus himself makes it clear that while it is
difficult it is not impossible for those who have wealth to
enter into the kingdom of God. There were, in fact,
wealthy persons who followed Jesus; as for instance Joseph
of Arimathea, a man whose riches served a good purpose,
for, being wealthy, he owned a tomb in which Jesus' body
could be interred.

The danger of wealth is not that it automatically excludes the one who possesses it from the kingdom, but that
it greatly strengthens the outer mask and inflates the ego.
By giving a man a feeling of power, influence, and regard
among men, it makes it difficult for him to achieve the inner
humility and admission of spiritual need which are prereq-
uisites to a genuine personality. As any counselor knows,
people with wealth can afford to perpetuate their neuroses,
alcoholism, and malingering far longer than those who
must serve men and life in order to make a livelihood.
Wealth easily becomes a prop behind which lurks a hollow,

hostile, or egocentric person. Nevertheless, it is not having wealth as such that destroys our relationship to the kingdom, but what it can do to us if we are unconscious of the dangers.

The listeners are truly shocked by what Jesus has to say about wealth. "In that case who can be saved?" they ask. In the mind of the time, as we saw earlier, the possession of wealth and good fortune generally was regarded as a sign of favor with God. In an attitude at least as old as the Book of Job, it was supposed that God, being just, would bestow blessings on the righteous and visit the unrighteous with misfortune, an attitude which did little for the cause of social justice. So if the wealthy could not be saved, then who could be saved? Again we see how radically Jesus cut across the collective ideas of his age. By seeing what was within man, he penetrated to the heart of things and transcended the attitudes of his time.

Identification with the outer mask effectively excludes us from the kingdom of God. On the other hand, sacrificing the outer mask—taking the risk of being oneself, whoever that may be—brings about the moment of salvation. This is beautifully illustrated in the story of Zacchaeus.

Zacchaeus was a tax collector and a wealthy man. Tax collectors became wealthy because they were allowed by the Romans to keep all the money they could collect over and above a certain fixed amount. Naturally this encouraged extortion and ruthlessness and attracted unscrupulous men, who were accordingly despised by the people

as the basest of sinners. Such a man was Zacchaeus. But
something had been stirring in Zacchaeus; and when Jesus
came to his village he wanted to see him, but couldn't because there was a big crowd and he was short of stature.
In order to get a glimpse of Jesus, Zacchaeus had to climb
into a sycamore tree, and there Jesus saw him.

'Zacchaeus, come down. Hurry, because I must stay at your
house today.' And he hurried down and welcomed him
joyfully (Luke 19:5–6).

The onlookers were horrified that Jesus would associate
with such a man. Again we must realize how shocking
Jesus' behavior was in the eyes of the people. There were
many righteous people who would gladly have had Jesus in
their homes that night, and here he had publicly chosen to
associate with the worst sinner in the village.

In the Gospel stories all the details are important. One
detail in this story which is a key to its meaning is the
sycamore tree, which, according to K. C. Pillai, was not
like our sycamore tree in the Occident, but was a mean and
lowly tree so despised that to have anything to do with it
was regarded as a disgrace. When Zacchaeus climbed in
public into the sycamore tree, he therefore completely sacrificed his outer mask. He publicly humiliated himself because he was so anxious to see this man of God. Jesus,
seeing him in the tree, knew that here was a man who was
ready for the kingdom of God. So after Zacchaeus vowed
to give half his property to the poor, and to return what he
had taken by extortion, Jesus was able to declare,

'Today salvation has come to this house, because this man too is a son of Abraham; for the Son of Man has come to seek out and save what was lost'. (Luke 19:9–10).

In our dreams the loss of the mask is sometimes represented as nakedness. When in our dreams we stand naked before others, it may be that we have lost our outer front so that we are psychologically naked or exposed. To be able to live among men "naked," without having to rely on an outer front, brings us close to the kingdom, as is clear from an interesting verse from the apocryphal Gospel According to Thomas:

His disciples said: When wilt Thou be revealed to us and when will we see thee? Jesus said: When you take off your clothing without being ashamed, and take your clothes and put them under your feet as the little children and tread on them, then shall you behold the Son of the Living One and you shall not fear (Gospel According to Thomas, Logion 37).

This reference to the little children's being naked helps us understand why Jesus so often referred to those who enter the kingdom of God as little children. When the disciples tried to stop some little children from coming to him, Jesus said,

'Let the little children alone, and do not stop them coming to me; for it is to such as these that the kingdom of heaven belongs' (Matthew 19:14/Luke 18:16/Mark 10:14).

Little children have no mask. Not until an adult world
forces it upon them by approving of one side of their
personality and disapproving of the other do children learn
to adopt a false front and hide their true feelings. Little
children are still spontaneous and express directly what
they feel with no hypocritical intention of producing a
desired effect. This is one of the several characteristics of
the small child which the adult must cultivate, in a mature
fashion, if he wishes to belong to the kingdom.

For the same psychological reasons we have discussed,
Jesus condemns the taking of oaths. An oath is necessary
only if the inner man contradicts the outer man. An oath
reinforces the strength of what we have outwardly prom-
ised or asserted, but this is necessary only if we are saying
what we do not mean; that is, if we are in a state of
contradiction. But for a member of the kingdom there is no
inner contradiction since the inner man and the outer man
are in relationship with each other. So Jesus says in the
Sermon on the Mount,

'Again, you have learnt how it was said to our ancestors:
You must not break your oath, but must fulfil your oaths to
the Lord. But I say this to you: do not swear at all, either by
heaven, since that is God's throne; or by the earth, since that
is his footstool; or by Jerusalem, since that is the city of the
great king. Do not swear by your own head either, since
you cannot turn a single hair white or black. All you need
say is "Yes" if you mean yes, "No" if you mean no; anything more than this comes from the evil one' (Matthew
5:33–37).

On the other hand, to persist in identifying with the mask is to foster a split within ourselves. Then the house of our soul is divided against itself and cannot stand. For

'Every kingdom divided against itself is heading for ruin; and no town, no household divided against itself can stand' (Matthew 12:25/Luke 11:17/Mark 3:24–25).

This saying may obviously be taken outwardly. It is a fact that no nation or household which is divided against itself can hope to withstand the tests of history. But the state of our own being is also a "house"; and if this inner house is inhabited by one who opposes our conscious self and our conscious intentions, our lives and the fabric of our personalities will not be able to stand either.

The kingdom of God requires that the outer man and the inner man correspond to each other. It is of no avail to cultivate an outer personality if it is not founded upon awareness of our inner selves, for no matter what we strive to accomplish outwardly in our lives, no matter what pretensions we make to righteousness, the actual fruit of our lives will be brought into existence from what is within our hearts. For,

'Make a tree sound and its fruit will be sound; make a tree rotten and its fruit will be rotten. For the tree can be told by its fruit' (Matthew 12:33/Luke 6:43–44)

and

'Can you not see that whatever goes into the mouth passes through the stomach and is discharged into the sewer? But the things that come out of the mouth come from the heart, and it is these that make a man unclean. For from the heart come evil intentions: murder, adultery, fornication, theft, perjury, slander. These are the things that make a man unclean. But to eat with unwashed hands does not make a man unclean' (Matthew 15:17–20).

It is not a matter of becoming a person who has no "shadowy" or "dark" thoughts or feelings. All of us have murderous thoughts, adulterous feelings, and the like from time to time. It is a matter of not leaving them "in the heart"; that is, not burying them in the unconscious. Once we recognize our thoughts and feelings for what they are, they are no longer "in the heart" but are brought out into the open. We may lose some of our moral self-esteem in this way, but we also lose our mask and gain moral humility. We then no longer live just by the Law, for we have confronted the one within us for whom the Law was necessary in the first place, and this lifts our whole personality to a higher moral plane.

This brings us to the next step of discipleship in the kingdom. Shedding the mask necessarily means confronting something in ourselves that is unpleasant and that we do not like. This is why we put on the mask in the first place. This unwanted side to our personalities we sense as our "enemy" as long as we are identified with the mask we wear. In reality the enemy is our unconsciousness which has caused us to identify with something false, but that is not the way we see it at first. Initially it looks as though we need our mask in order to hide from a dreadful inner adversary. So it is appropriate that next we turn to consider "the inner adversary."

6

The
Inner
Adversary

✠✠✠

            The first proclamation concerning the kingdom of God is "Repent, for the kingdom of heaven is close at hand" (Matthew 3:2, 4:17/Mark 1:15). This "repentance" comes from the Greek word "metanoia," which means not so much being sorry for what we have done as it does "turning about," a complete reversal of oneself and of one's life. The translation "repent" fails to carry the psychological impact of Jesus' saying. Understood as a "turnabout," metanoia includes turning away from our identification with our outer masks, and confronting what lies behind that mask: what looks like an inner adversary or enemy.

            We have always known that we have enemies. What we have seldom realized is that each of us also carries an adversary within ourself. This adversary is the person within us who contradicts the outer front. He is the one who thinks the thoughts we do not want to acknowledge as our own, who has feelings and urges we dare not openly express because to do so would throw into jeopardy the role and image we have assumed for ourselves. He is the one we try,

111

usually unsuccessfully, to hide from others, out of fear that they will reject us, and also to hide from ourselves, because we think we could not stand to face him. He is the Mr. Hyde to our Dr. Jekyll, the one who manages to bring about some evil in spite of our pretensions to virtue or, more passively, the one who stands between us and our goals or ideals and prevents our achieving them.

The relationship between the inner enemy and the mask is one of diametrical opposition. The more we are identified with a mask, the more the unconscious will set up an opposing viewpoint in the form of the inner enemy. The more we pretend to be this or that, the more the enemy will be the opposite. Therefore, it is only as we become conscious of the mask we wear that we can hope to make peace with ourselves. As we shall see more clearly later on, the term "enemy" is somewhat of a misnomer. This part of our personality *seems* like our enemy as long as we are identified with a false image of ourselves. Our *real* enemy is our unconsciousness of the mask we are wearing. This unconsciousness must be overcome if we are to come to terms with ourselves and be open to the new creative life of the kingdom.

If we have long denied the inner enemy and then finally see him, it may be a crushing experience as all the self-loathing and inner rejection of ourselves come to the surface. "I saw myself and I did not like what I saw," recently cried a woman who had buried her true feelings out of fear of being hurt, and had assumed a false role in life which she had lived to the destruction of herself and her relationship to her husband.

The inner enemy will frequently appear in our dreams as

a figure of the same sex as the dreamer. One man dreams of him as the black man who must be hung. A minister dreams of him as a faithless beatnik. A man with a great power drive may dream of him as the weak one. He may appear as a bum, a crippled or maimed person, a highly conventional, pasteboard person, or a harlot, or simply as a lurking unknown figure or as someone wanting to kill us. In the case of a hardened criminal, a person dedicated to hate, he may appear as a positive figure, a gentle, loving person; for the inner enemy is neither good nor bad in himself, but is that within us which contradicts whatever conscious attitude we have adopted.

So reluctant are men to see themselves as they really are and to face their inner contradiction that it is only by the greatest of efforts that most people can be brought to this self-confrontation. The vast majority prefer the wide way of unconsciousness which leads to ignorance of the inner enemy. This is destructive because ignorance of the inner enemy by no means resolves the problem. To the contrary, the enemy now appears in the guise of other people, and the hostility which has its origin in ourselves takes the form of hostility to others.

Whatever we have ignored which is vital and important to our total personality is seen in others. This "projection" of something in ourselves onto others is done quite unconsciously on our part, which is why we always seem so innocent in our own eyes. The projection of our enemy onto another individual distorts our relationship with him and forces that person to carry a psychological burden which is most unfair to him.

Sometimes this is done with children. One rigid, moralis-

tic woman projected onto her daughter all her own unrecognized sensuality. From puberty on, the girl was casti-
gated as a worthless slut, a whore in the making. It was no
surprise when at the age of sixteen the girl became pregnant
out of marriage. To the mother, it was a corroboration of
what she had known all along. For the daughter it was a
fate forced upon her by the projection of her mother's own
shadowy nature, which she had been forced to carry and to
live out.

The projection of the adversary may be on races as well
as on individuals, and, because the word "blackness" is
often used to describe a morally dubious side of ourselves
which we hate and fear, it is sometimes projected by the
white man onto the black man, who then quite unfairly
must carry the white man's shadow. The white man then
tends to see an enemy in the black man, to sense in him
qualities that he finds objectionable in himself. The black
man's sexuality is exaggerated when he carries the projection of the white man's own desires. The black man's joy-
fulness and spontaneity are misread as irresponsibility or
childishness by a white man no longer in touch with his
own emotions and urges. But the projection may also take
the other direction, and the black man may project onto
the white man certain frustrations the sources of which
are in himself. Now the white man may be blamed for
holding negative attitudes toward the black man which, in
fact, the black man holds toward himself, or may be held
responsible for holding the black man down, when in reality the black man is held down from within by his own
feelings of inferiority or self-rejection.

When the projection of our inner enemy onto another

takes place on a collective, racial, or international basis, it is always particularly destructive. The Nazis were an example. Having identified themselves as a superrace and a divinely superior people, they were no longer able to recognize their own inferior qualities. The hidden, inferior qualities in them were therefore seen in the Jews. The Jews had to carry for the Nazis what they would not see in themselves. They carried the burden of the hate and fear and loathing which, in fact, the Nazis had for themselves. The ensuing wholesale and horrible slaughter of the Jews was a futile attempt by the Nazis to exterminate their projected inner enemy.

The beginning of the solution to the problem of the enemy is to recognize him within ourselves. We carry the enemy in our own hearts. We hate him because he contradicts us. We fear that if we acknowledge him as our own he will take us over completely. The precise opposite is true. *Not* to acknowledge him is to fall into the power of the inner enemy who mocks our futile efforts to get rid of him by getting rid of those who carry the projected burden of our own darkness. To acknowledge him as our own is to begin to be released from his power and to find his constructive side.

For the recognition of the inner enemy has a transforming effect upon us. It necessarily causes us to relinquish an identification with our mask and to accept our reality as a person. This in itself reduces the enmity between the inner enemy and the conscious personality, for the seeming enmity of the former is largely dependent on the identification which we have with our Pharasaic front. The inner enemy includes essential parts of ourselves which have

been excluded from our conscious personality development. Now they can be included in the conscious personality instead of being relegated to the hell of being split
off in the unconscious. With this coming into consciousness, a further transformation in the inner enemy is now
seen. Whatever it was we feared in ourselves can now show
its inner "gold," for that which in the eyes of consciousness
may have seemed dreadful, in the eyes of God belongs
to us and holds some ingredient which is essential to our
wholeness. Like the frog in the fairy tale which was transformed into a handsome prince when the princess accepted
him as her partner in bed, so the inner enemy is transformed
into a useful part of the personality *once it has been consciously recognized and accepted as a legitimate and inevitable part of ourselves.*

For as we will see in the next chapter, it is not the enemy
who is evil but our unawareness of him which creates evil.
The enemy within contradicts us as long as we do not
acknowledge him but, recognized and accepted, he com-
plements us rather than contradicts us, and what before
seemed exclusively negative properties now show their positive side. It takes great spiritual courage to recognize our
inner division and see the enemy. But there can be no
entrance into the kingdom of God without this act of
"metanoia."

$$\oplus$$

Jesus knows of the inner enemy and the need to be
reconciled with him. So he says in the Sermon on the
Mount,

'Come to terms with your opponent in good time while you are still on the way to the court with him, or he may hand you over to the judge and the judge to the officer, and you will be thrown into prison. I tell you solemnly, you will not get out till you have paid the last penny' (Matthew 5:25–26/Luke 12:57–59).

In ancient times courts were located only in the major cities. In order to go to the court, it was necessary for most people to travel some distance, and it was the custom for the entire party concerned in the case to travel together. Happily, they might settle the case en route and not have to trouble the authorities.

At first glance it looks as though Jesus is simply recommending that lawsuits be settled out of court. But this piece of advice, while usually commendable, is hardly brilliant, nor would it always be the right thing to do since, in some cases, perhaps a matter should be brought to the court. Moreover, it is clear that Jesus had more than this in mind, for if we do *not* come to terms with our opponent, *we*, not he, will be held to account for it. If this is a literal lawsuit with an outer opponent, there is no reason why we should always be the ones to be held guilty. But if this is an *inner* opponent, we *will* be held to account if we do not become reconciled with him. For it is the task of consciousness to recognize, face, and be reconciled with every aspect of our total self. If we fail to do so, we have to reckon with the larger authority within us—that is, with the court of the King—and we then must pay a bitter price by experiencing in a negative way what we have denied.

St. Augustine has some very instructive things to say about this particular passage. If we are sinning, says St.

Augustine, "The Word of God is thine adversary. . . . It
is the adversary of thy will till it becomes the author of thy
salvation. . . . It is our adversary *as long as we are our
own adversaries. As long as thou art thine own enemy, thou
hast the word of God thine enemy; be thine own friend,
and thou art in agreement with it"* (Sermon LIX; italics
mine). Here Augustine sees not only the inner meaning of
the passage—that this adversary is ourself—but also the
mysterious connection between the adversary and God. As
we shall learn shortly, by dealing with our inner opponent,
dark and undesirable though he may seem, we find ourselves also dealing with God.

Another example of the same motif is the well-known
Parable of the Prodigal Son (Luke 15:11–32). The
younger son is a roguish, pleasure-seeking spendthrift. The
older son is duty-bound, self-righteous, unforgiving, and
joyless. Taken as outer figures, they refer to two types of
people: the pleasure-seeking and the superresponsible. The
emphasis would then be on the forgiving and reconciling
power of God, exemplified in the Father, and it would be a
kind of morality parable on the evils of pleasure-seeking
and the need to forgive and to accept others.

However, when taken as inner figures, the two brothers
represent two halves of one whole personality. Some of us
may identify with the older-brother side of ourselves and
are ruled by a strong sense of duty, a desire to conform
and to please, and to appear righteous. We then drive the
younger-brother side of ourselves into the unconscious
where he becomes our inner enemy and not only opposes
our conscious attitudes but robs us of our joy of life, our
compassion for others, and our spontaneity. Others may

identify with the wayward son and drive their responsible side into the unconscious. They then lead a life which seeks pleasure, but are continually opposed from within by their own repressed conscience. While they seemingly derive enjoyment from life, it is always deranged pleasure.

As long as the two brothers are divided against each other, one defeats the other. But if the two brothers can be conjoined into one personality so that the inner opposition is ended, wholeness can appear, and the negative qualities of each brother will give way to his positive qualities. The older-brother side will lend mature responsibility and conscience to the younger brother, and the younger-brother side will add humor, joy, compassion, and spontaneity to the older brother.

It is this reconciliation which the Father, who represents here the kingdom of God, tries to bring about. The moment for redemption could occur when the younger brother "came to himself" (Luke 15:17 KJV; Jerusalem Bible has "came to his senses")—that is, confronted himself and his own one-sidedness. This self-confrontation must also occur with the older brother. In the Parable he tries to avoid it by referring in conversation with the Father to "this thy son" (verse 30 KJV). But the father brings him back to the need for his own self-confrontation, his own need to accept the prodigal as his other half, with the words,

'Son, thou art ever with me, and all that I have is thine. It was meet that we should make merry, and be glad: for this *thy brother* was dead, and is alive again; and was lost, and is found' (Luke 15:31-32 KJV; italics mine).

Such an acceptance of our inner opponent as a legitimate part of our total personality is possible only if we first recognize him. This recognition cannot take place so long as the inner opponent is projected onto others, for in this way he is invisible to us as a part of ourselves. The withdrawal of projections is therefore a very important part of the ethic of the kingdom of God, for only in this way do we become conscious of what is our own, and only in this way can we be released from the bondage in which men are caught through their projections. The withdrawal of our projections is the motif underlying many of the sayings of Jesus which speak to the attitude we are to have toward others, because only then can we relate to others as individuals and be free from compulsive enslavement to our own unconsciousness.

> 'You have learnt how it was said to our ancestors: *You must not kill;* and if anyone does kill he must answer for it before the court. But I say this to you: anyone who is angry with his brother will answer for it before the court; if a man calls his brother "Fool" he will answer for it before the Sanhedrin; and if a man calls him "Renegade" he will answer for it in hell fire' (Matthew 5:21–22).

The terms which Jesus warns us against using are sweeping in their condemnation. "Fool" and "renegade" imply a total rejection of the personality of the other person. This kind of total rejection of another—the total dehumanization of personality—is a characteristic occurrence when someone else is carrying the burden of our own darkness. A person who is carrying the burden of our projections is no longer human to us. He becomes in our eyes devilish, sinister, a nonperson. This is why we are so prone to become angry with these people, since they are no longer people but represent to us what angers us in ourselves.

This may be why St. Paul says, "Let not the sun go down upon your wrath" (Ephesians 4:26 KJV). The sun is the light of consciousness. If we are angry, we are not to let this emotion possess us without becoming conscious of the sources of our anger. Generally these sources may be found in our own unconscious weaknesses which another person has probed successfully, or in our hatred of the inner opponent, which by our projections we are forcing someone else to carry. Such unconsciousness distorts our relationship both to others and to ourselves so completely that it is no longer possible to relate to God. So Jesus continues,

'So then, if you are bringing your offering to the altar and there remember that your brother has something against you, leave your offering there before the altar, go and be reconciled with your brother first, and then come back and present your offering' (Matthew 5:23–24).

Notice that here, as in the case of the opponent with whom we must be reconciled while we are on the way to the court, the burden of responsibility is on us. The task of the ego is to become conscious. If there is enmity with our brother ("your brother has something against you"), the job before us is to become conscious of the sources of this enmity. Otherwise we are ruled by darkness, we fall under the power of sin, and, as we shall see in Chapter 7, we fall prey to evil. So before we can come to God, we must resolve this unconscious relationship; then we can come to the altar with our gift.

The same motif is struck in Jesus' words about judgment of others,

> 'Do not judge, and you will not be judged; because the judgements you give are the judgements you will get, and the amount you measure out is the amount you will be given' (Matthew 7:1–2/Luke 6:37).

Jesus does not mean that we should not evaluate others. Anyone who seeks to make a friend, who must employ someone else or work for someone else, or who is doing business with others, must evaluate other people. Judgment is different from evaluating because judgment is final. When we judge someone, we have subjected him to a blanket condemnation. We have assumed a godlike role to him because in judging him we claim to know the meaning and moral consequences of his life. In so doing, we violate his individuality. This inflates us with a false sense of our superiority at the expense of the humanity of the other person. Judging others is always dehumanizing; and it is an example of our inflation as well, since it depends on our presumptuous assumption that we are in a position to pass judgment on the life and soul of another.

Evaluating another person can rest upon an objective appraisal of another person's character or personality. Judging another person rests upon our own unconsciousness, and this is why Jesus condemns it. Because judgment of others is finalistic, the element of projection always occurs. It is because we see in the other person what we hate in ourselves that our judgment is such an unconscious act.

This is why our judgment of others always returns to us, since in judging them we are, in effect, judging ourselves. The total rejection involved in judgment is based ultimately upon a rejection of something in ourselves of which we are unconscious. There is a virtual law of the psyche that the unconscious turns to consciousness the same face which consciousness has adopted toward the unconscious. This is often seen in our dreams. If we are running from ourselves, the unconscious figures will be pursuing us; if we turn and face them, the whole relationship will change. If we hate and fear something in ourselves, it will appear dreadful and evil; but if we accept it, the fearfulness will disappear. If we are a man who has rejected his feminine side, it will appear as a vindictive, slighted woman; but if accepted, she appears supportive and loving. So with judgment. If we judge others, it is because we are judging something in ourselves of which we are unaware. The judgment then returns to us in the form of a condemnation of consciousness on the part of the unconscious. This is why Jesus says,

> 'because the judgements you give are the judgements you will get, and the amount you measure out is the amount you will be given.'

It is not a matter of God's keeping records of what we do and giving us back tit for tat; it is a spiritual law. Just as we will surely become ill if we take poison into our body, so we will surely incur inner judgment if we stand in judgment on others.

It is on this basis that Jesus is able to urge us to love our enemies:

'You have learnt how it was said: You must love your neighbour and hate your enemy. But I say this to you: love your enemies and pray for those who persecute you; in this way you will be sons of your Father in heaven, for he causes his sun to rise on bad men as well as good, and his rain to fall on honest and dishonest men alike. For if you love those who love you, what right have you to claim any credit? Even the tax collectors do as much, do they not? And if you save your greetings for your brothers, are you doing anything exceptional? Even the pagans do as much, do they not?' (Matthew 5:43–47/Luke 6:27–36).

This radical new interpretation of how we should relate to our enemies is perhaps the most controversial of all Jesus' teachings because it seems to be the most impossible. Certainly it is one of the least practiced. It always seems so natural, so justifiable to men that they should have enemies and should hate them that the words of Jesus in this regard are studiously ignored.

There are many reasons why Jesus urges us not to hate our enemies. If we do so, we can never rise to any kind of moral superiority. Man has always loved his friends and hated his enemies. If we do this, what right have we to claim any moral superiority to the lowest of men? But if we love our enemies we can begin to be sons of the Father; that is, to reflect in ourselves that sonship with the Creator which comes to those who are rising above the natural unconsciousness of man to a moral life founded upon consciousness of oneself.

The only spiritual way to resist evil is to become so conscious of what is involved that we can avoid becoming part of the evil situation. For the danger in hating one's enemy is, as Laurens van der Post has pointed out, that *men tend to become like what they oppose.* This is why it is necessary that if we would belong to the kingdom of God, we be supremely conscious when dealing with our enemies. Hatred, moreover, will bind us to that which we hate, for as long as we are in a state of hatred toward a person or a people, we are enslaved. That is why those who would belong to the kingdom must go beyond the life of hatred into the life of consciousness. Only then can we be free to enter into the kingdom as sons of the Father.

Forsaking an identification with our Pharasaic front means a confrontation with the inner enemy, and confrontation with the enemy can lead to acceptance and reconciliation, so that where before there were two opposed to each other, now there is harmony. But this will involve a radical transformation in the way we think about ourselves. For the sake of our own relationship to the kingdom, as well as for the sake of our relationships with other people, our attitude toward ourself must be one of self-acceptance.

This comes as something of a shock to people who have often been trained to reject themselves. Centuries of indoctrination that we are sinners, that evil springs from man, and that a large part of our personality is to be regarded as belonging to the devil, have inevitably made a fetish out of the idea of self-rejection. For many, the Christian life is

identical with a life in which one places no value what-
soever upon oneself, where one is supposed to efface one's
self completely, placing value only on others and on God.
But now it appears that those who would belong to the
kingdom are expected to strive for self-acceptance, and this
even involves acceptance of parts of our personality which
seem to be of the lowest, most inferior or devilish sort.
Small wonder that the elder brother objected to the idea
that he must welcome his younger brother home! How can
we accept *this* part of ourselves, this shameful, or worthless,
or weak, or retarded person we would much prefer not to
acknowledge as our own?

It begins to become clear that the ethic of the kingdom
of God is more paradoxical than we have ever dared let
ourselves suppose. The man who becomes a son of the
Father is not, after all, going to be the "pure" man, but will
be a man whose growing knowledge and acceptance of
himself have developed in him a unique capacity for love.
Not righteousness but love, not following rules but conscious self-acceptance, are the keys to the kingdom of God.
So Jesus, when asked to name the greatest of the commandments, says,

> 'You must love the Lord your God with all your heart, with
> all your soul, and with all your mind. This is the greatest and
> the first commandment. The second resembles it: You must
> love your neighbour *as yourself*' (Matthew 22:37–39; ital-
> ics mine).

Pauline had spent forty years striving to fulfill the moral
demands which she had been told were part of the Christian life. Faithfully she listened to parents, church, and

friends exhort her to goodness, and describe to her the kind of person she must be in order to be acceptable to God. Moved by a touching sincerity and need for approval, she strove with all her might to fill the role apparently expected of her by God, only to find her own personality shrinking and shrinking until at last there was so little of herself left that she could barely function. At this point the creative aspect of herself, so long crushed, rebelled, and she was so victimized and driven by anxiety that she was compelled to seek help. Gradually over many months she saw how she had spent half a lifetime trying to live up to the standards not of God, but of men, and in so doing had failed to realize her creative self.

Her own self was a stranger to her at first, and she had to get to know her. As she came to see herself, she saw her inner enemy, the part of her which simply would not, and could not, fit into the image prescribed for her by others. This was the woman within her whom she had to recognize, then accept, then love, so that she could become the person she was created to be by God. The only road left for her as a way out of her anxiety was to know herself so that she could love herself. This road also set her on the path to the kingdom of God, toward a life with a promise of creativity and spontaneity. The person who began to emerge in her as her true self was no one-sided saint. She had to recognize and accept an amoral instinctual side and many negative feelings, as well as her positive feeling side. Yet she was fulfilling the admonition Jesus gave,

'You must therefore be perfect just as your heavenly Father is perfect' (Matthew 5:48).

There is probably no saying of Jesus subjected to more abuse than this one. The very way in which it is translated into our English Bibles does violence to its profound and paradoxical meaning, for "you must therefore be perfect" brings to our minds the image of abiding by a perfectionist moral code which allows us no shadow, no taint of impurity or imperfection; in short, which does not allow us any possibility for reconciliation with the inner enemy. But this is a misleading translation, for, as we saw earlier, the Greek word rendered "perfect" means literally "brought to an end state." It is not a matter of achieving some impossible and inhuman saintlike condition, but of being fulfilled as the person we were created to be. We are to be complete or whole, our lives and personalities brought to the conclusion which God has intended, and not to become perfect in the narrow and one-sided meaning of the word. It is this completeness, this paradoxical wholeness, which is the goal of the kingdom of God, and it can be established only in persons whose very faults and failures have contributed to the development within them of their highest potential and greatest capacity for love. Such a person will not be other-worldly, but this-worldly; he will not have fled from involvement with the things of the world, but will be involved with the world, and yet will not have succumbed to the collective values of the world. This person will be, in Jesus' words,

> 'cunning as serpents and yet as harmless as doves' (Matthew 10:16).

He will be wise as a serpent because, like the serpent, he will be familiar with the things of the earth. Yet he will be innocent as a dove because he will be *conscious of his own motives* and his own earth-nature, and in this way will remain innocent. Such a person's wholeness will be extremely paradoxical. Among the radical descriptions of such a person are the Parable of the Crafty Steward (Luke 16:1–8) and the story of the woman who was a sinner (Luke 7:36–50).

The crafty steward has been discovered by his master to have been wasteful with his property, so that the master determines to release him. The steward at first does not know what to do. He is not strong enough to work with his body; he cannot bring himself to go begging. Finally he hits upon a plan. Going to his master's debtors, he settles with them one by one, in each case clearing their accounts with the master for somewhat less than the full amount which they owe. In this way he wins their favor so that when he is dismissed he will have a place to go. Jesus concludes the parable with these surprising words:

'The master praised the dishonest steward for his astuteness. For the children of this world are more astute in dealing with their own kind than are the children of light' (Luke 16:8).

The children of this world are out only for their own self-interest; yet they demonstrate a commendable astuteness in dealing with the world. The children of light are those who seek a life which may be lived in the light of God, but they too are to be astute in the dealings with the world.

Equally paradoxical is the story of the woman who was a

sinner. One of the Pharisees had invited Jesus to a meal, but while Jesus was there a woman entered who was widely known for her bad reputation. Yet she so loved Jesus that she wept over him, and, as her tears fell on his feet, she wiped them with her hair. The Pharisee was shocked at seeing this and said to himself,

'If this man were a prophet, he would know who this woman is that is touching him and what a bad name she has' (Luke 7:39).

But Jesus, knowing what thoughts were going through his mind, pointed out to him the great debt which had been forgiven her, and the great love which she showed. He then concluded with this paradoxical statement,

'For this reason I tell you that her sins, her many sins, must have been forgiven her, or she would not have shown such great love. *It is the man who is forgiven little who shows little love*' (Luke 7:47; italics mine).

And turning to the woman, he said,

'Your faith has saved you; go in peace' (verse 50).

We have here more than a story in forgiveness. It is not just that God is willing to forgive a sinner who is repentant, for the woman who wiped Jesus' feet with her tears because of the forgiveness of her sins showed *more* love than did the Pharisee who had no reason (in his own mind at least) to be forgiven. What is meant is that we are to *live intensely*, even if this means we can no longer avoid blame.

The Pharisee, by always playing it safe, sought to remain blameless before God, but as a result he was not emotionally involved with life and people as was the woman who was a sinner. She found greater love than the Pharisee and she was made whole, for in spite of her sins she had *lived*.

Such a view of the life of the kingdom of God is disturbing to puritanical minds and consciences which have for so long been Pharisaic in their attitudes, because it raises the question of the role of evil and of the nature of sin. What is evil? What is sin? The Pharisees had some ideas about evil and sin which apparently Jesus did not share. What Jesus' ideas of sin and evil were, and how they fit into the message of the kingdom of God, are the next topics to which we must turn.

7

The Role of Evil and Sin in the Way

✠ ✠ ✠

One traditional ecclesiastical attitude toward the problem of evil is that it does not really exist. In its own right it can't exist, for if it did God would be responsible for it; and since God must be good, evil cannot be. What seems to be evil has no existence in its own right as a metaphysical principle in opposition to good, but derives its existence as a deprivation of the good. God created the world entirely good; only insofar as the creation falls short of the perfection God gave it does evil come into being.

According to this view, free will is the chief instrument in this decline from perfection which leads to evil. Men bring about evil by choosing to disobey God. In so doing, they fall away from God and by their disobedient choice create evil. In this way God is relieved of any responsibility for the existence of evil, since free will itself is a valuable

132

good. Thus "all good to God and all evil to man" becomes the maxim.

The psychological consequence of this theory of the origin of evil is the burdening of man with an extreme sense of guilt. Since man can create evil, where by its own substance alone it could have no existence, man becomes endowed with a Luciferian power. As a result, man feels both a sense of power that he can create evil in his own right, and a sense of overwhelming guilt, since everything evil that occurs is due to him.

The ethical consequence of this theory is that evil can be overcome only in the same way that it was started: by man's choosing obedience rather than disobedience. Man is, according to this theory, supposed to be a rational creature who has it in his power to make this choice. Man's will must thus be appealed to, to choose the good; if he fails to do so, it is because of his deliberate ill will, and he should accordingly be punished. Theologically this punishment is meted out in hell, where man receives from God everlasting punishment for temporal sins. Socially this same code of punishment is reflected in our penal codes, which assume that men have the power to choose between good and evil and so should receive punishment if they choose the way of disobedience.

This view of evil is religiously dangerous because it tends to minimize the power of evil. It may be this doctrine—that evil is only the deprivation of good—which has caused the Church to fail to develop an effective means of combating evil here on earth. It is philosophically inadequate because everything which has been asserted of evil could also be asserted of good; good could also be defined as only the deprivation of evil, as well as the other way around. Psychologically the theory is inadequate because it ignores the facts of human nature. Men do not always have the power to choose their actions. Often as not they are relatively helpless in the face of enormously destructive forces of which they are unconscious. Socially this theory of evil is inadequate because it fails to recognize that the moral failure of the life of any one person is also a reflection on the inadequacy of the entire society.

It is important to observe that this is not the idea of evil held by Jesus. For Jesus, evil existed in its own right. There was no question about its reality; it was an independent autonomous agency opposed to God. Jesus himself confronted the powers of evil in his temptations in the wilderness. He referred often to Satan as the personification of the autonomous spiritual evil. His healing miracles were largely directed against the forces of evil, since the maladies he healed were regarded by him as forms of demonic possession against which the individual was quite helpless.

Man did not create evil by his own choice, for evil existed on its own. Man might choose to follow good or evil; his actions might lay him open to possession by the evil one. Man's choices *were* quite crucial, but they did not create an evil which previously was not there. To the contrary, the inner world of man was filled with spiritual or psychological powers making for evil, powers which could possess a person and so thoroughly control him that only the power of God could bring release.

Jesus does not tell us why God tolerates the existence of evil in Creation, but he does tell us that God knows about the existence of evil. In the Lord's Prayer we are admonished to pray,

'Lead us not into temptation, but deliver us from evil'
(Matthew 6:13 KJV/Luke 11:4 KJV; Matthew 6:13 in the
Jerusalem Bible has "the evil one").

As mentioned earlier, Jesus points out that

'he [God] causes his sun to rise on bad men as well as good,
and his rain to fall on honest and dishonest men alike'
(Matthew 5:45).

In speaking of his forthcoming betrayal by Judas, he speaks
of the necessity for the evil of the betrayal, yet warns
against the fate which befalls those who come to serve the
purposes of evil:

'The Son of Man does indeed go to his fate even as it has
been decreed, but alas for that man by whom he is be-
trayed!' (Luke 22:22/Matthew 26:24/Mark 14:21).

These passages suggest that evil may be a necessity. It is,
in fact, hard to visualize a spiritual world which has any
moral significance without there being powers both of
good and of evil. Psychologically, man's consciousness
grows primarily through opposition to evil; men become
conscious out of necessity in order to overcome evil. It is
only consciousness and love which enable us to avoid the
snares of the Evil One, so that in some paradoxical way evil
may serve a deep, ultimate purpose of God. If this be so,

the solution to the problem of evil is no longer to identify
God with the good. God is beyond good and evil as men
know them; good and evil are the two polarities necessary
if there is to be any spiritual or moral meaning to Creation.

This seems to be the philosophy of evil underlying Jesus'
warning to Peter that he will deny Jesus at the time of his
arrest:

> 'Simon, Simon! Satan, you must know, has got his wish to
> sift you all like wheat; but I have prayed for you, Simon,
> that your faith may not fail, and once you have recovered,
> you in your turn must strengthen your brothers' (Luke
> 22:31–32).

This passage reminds us of the Prologue to the Book of
Job, where Satan is allowed by God to try to subvert Job's
faithfulness and loyalty (Chapters 1 and 2). In the Book of
Job Satan acts like God's own doubting thought. In Peter's
case Satan works through Peter's doubting thought regarding Jesus, a thought which plays upon Peter's fears for
himself. In this saying Jesus seems to recognize that there is
an adverse power which has divine permission to operate in
the world with a certain autonomy. The same idea seems to
underlie Jesus' remark to his disciples in the Garden of
Gethsemane just as he goes into agonized prayer over his
forthcoming crucifixion,

> 'Pray not to be put to the test' (Luke 22:40).

This reminds us of the Lord's Prayer, which has the
exhortation "Lead us not into temptation." The implica-
tion seems to be that God Himself may put us to the test,

and that under the strain of the test we may fall victim to evil. Certainly without the existence of evil, there can be no such thing as a spiritual test. In fact, without evil there can be no such thing as a consciousness at all in a moral or spiritual sense.

Sensing the necessity of evil for the advancement of spiritual consciousness, some psychologists have ventured into the outskirts of the fields of philosophy and theology and have asserted that evil also belongs to the ultimate wholeness of things. C. G. Jung in particular repeatedly intimated that totality must include evil as well as good. This is a dangerous and misleading thought for, in spite of the necessity for evil, *evil has a negative power of its own which is directly opposed to the life-giving power of totality.* We must distinguish between chaotic or undifferentiated parts of our personality, which may seem to us to be devilish but which must be included if we are to be whole, and absolute or ultimate evil—a very different thing which cannot be integrated into wholeness since it is antiwholeness. The evil of the mass executions by the Nazis, or of rampant murder, or of a total personality breakdown is not an evil that can be accepted or integrated. Psychotherapists, as well as clergy, join instinctively in combating evil of this kind.

Man can only oppose and seek to avoid or overcome this form of evil, because it stands in fundamental opposition to wholeness. This is not the darkness which must be included with the light to form a totality. This is an expression of an evil so numinous and destructive that it is fundamentally in opposition to wholeness. It is antiself, antiwholeness, anti-Christ and though it may, in some ultimate sense man cannot fathom, serve the deepest purposes of God, it remains man's task to combat it resolutely and consciously, as did Jesus himself.

From an experiential point of view, evil may be described as the power which works for dissociation; it exists specifically wherever a part seeks to take over the whole. A good example in the physical realm is cancer, in which rampant malignant cells seek to take over a total organism, and, if they succeed, bring death. In the psychological realm such a process may be seen in disintegrative psychoses which destroy the unity of personality and dissolve it into unrelated fragments. Another example of psychological evil is the domination of the ego by some autonomous aspect of the personality, which leads to a kind of possession which nullifies the power to make choices. In such cases we have a person in whom the conscious life is so dominated by a split-off part of the unconscious personality that the term "demon possession" is descriptively accurate.

The story of Helene is a good example. Helene, a young woman in her early twenties, was referred to me by another clergyman after several unsuccessful counseling attempts with members of various healing professions. Her chief complaints were violent moods in which she would throw things and become wildly angry, have suicidal impulses, feel strong dissatisfaction with her work as a teacher, and suffer a variety of physical symptoms chief of which was pain, especially down her left leg. Because of the physical complaints she had initially been referred to physicians, who, after thorough examinations, pronounced her physically well but emotionally disturbed and referred her to a psychologist for counseling. For one reason or another she had been unable to establish a rapport with this counselor, or with others to whom she was sent in turn, and wound up in my office.

Our work together fell into several distinct stages: an initial stage in which I sought to establish rapport, a subsequent stage in which we worked together to find a cause for her disorientation, a crisis, a resolution of the crisis, and the consolidation of a new personality structure. My first efforts were directed largely toward our relationship. I encouraged her to express freely her feelings about coming to see me, and about her situation in general. As I listened to her, I could sense in myself a feeling of inner connectedness to this person, a basic liking and strange confidence that I was destined to play a role in her life. Eventually a rapport was established, enabling us to search together as partners for the reasons for her personal distress and disorientation.

Our efforts in this regard were singularly unsuccessful. There were no traumas or conflicts, inner or outer, which seemed to suffice as an explanation for the deeply disturbing moods over which she had so little control. I was frankly alarmed, for I recognized the danger of suicide (there had already been one unsuccessful suicide attempt). I was also disturbed by the continuing physical symptoms and insisted that she maintain contact with her physician, with whom I consulted over the phone. Nothing we could theorize was more than an intellectualization, and only our rapport, and her desperation, kept the counseling process going.

Then the crisis came. There was a midnight phone call, a desperate voice on the other end of the line. She was alone, overwhelmed by a dark and Satanic mood, driven by a compulsion to do away with herself, subject to feelings of utter hopelessness. Carefully, slowly, patiently, I talked with her until I could feel her begin to return to herself. She was safe again, but only for the moment. The next day she came in to see me and we searched again for a precipitating cause for her extreme depression of the night before. None could be found. At last I asked her, "What would your mood look like if you painted it?" She had never painted before in her adult life, but immediately she began to wave her arms about, describing how it would look. I remembered one of my teachers once saying to me, "If someone waves his arms when telling a dream, it means it is supposed to be painted." "Go home and paint what you see in your mind," I said, "and return to me as soon as it is done."

The painting which this young woman did is one of the most remarkable I have ever seen for its psychological impact. She succeeded in recording in color, and in much black paint, the essence of her terrifying mood. The painting spoke more than a thousand words. She was completely gripped while doing this work, and when it was done she felt exhausted but enormously relieved. This painting broke the back of her depression. From this time on she was never again taken over by this Satanic darkness. A flood of material now poured forth from her inner world. Other paintings followed, and dreams appeared which we both began to understand. The grip of the powers of darkness over her had ended, and her recovery had begun.

Everything improved, that is, except the physical symptoms, and these got worse. By now she refused to return to her medical doctor, who attributed her symptoms to a supposed neurotic, malingering state of mind. But somehow I knew that the matter had to be settled once and for all. I had a friend who was a fine neurologist; surely he could help. An examination by this doctor showed what the previous physician had missed: a massive slipped disc pressing on the spinal column, sending darts of pain throughout her body. Surgery corrected the problem, and the physical cure also helped the psychological difficulty. Our work together progressed rapidly, and the desire to live and the urge to wholeness became stronger than the wish for destruction and death. Out of the chaos and disorientation there could now emerge a personality not only healthy but brilliant and creative, for the power over her of a Satanic darkness had been broken.

A second version of evil as possession of the whole by a part is seen in the power drive because of its unique capacity to enslave the ego. Personality is endowed with a drive for power, which under some circumstances serves a useful function as legitimate ambition, or as the incentive for the personal aggressiveness necessary to attainment in life. But in an egocentric personality in which the ego has identified itself, in godlike fashion, with totality, the power drive becomes demonic. An extreme example can be seen in the case of Adolf Hitler. More homely examples may include the neurotic woman who substitutes manipulation of others for relationship, or the man whose ambition becomes ruthlessness, or the powerful nation which becomes carried away and inflated by its own sense of power and tries to achieve by force goals which accord with its own philosophy.

A minister I know was once quite startled by a dream in which he was walking hand in hand in a companionate and friendly way with a sinister figure with yellow eyes and a devious manner. Upon reflecting on the dream, he recalled that the day before he had been asked by a highly respected colleague to do a special favor, a favor which amounted to an acknowledgement on his colleague's part of a need for his "superior" wisdom and skill. The experience had inflated the minister. Without realizing it at the time, he had been carried away by an exaggerated sense of his own importance. On recalling this, he realized that the sinister figure in his dream was himself. It is descriptively accurate to say that the devil had entered the picture through the minister's unconscious power drive which would have subtly taken him over had he not been helped by the dream to see what was happening.

It is because the ego is susceptible to the power drive that it has acquired an unsavory reputation. Yet it is not the ego itself which is evil, but its possession by the power complex. The ego is an absolutely essential part of man's personality. Without an ego there can be no personality, nor can there be a recognition of God; so the ego is very necessary to God as well as to man. Far from being intrinsically evil, the ego is capable of making supreme sacrifices and of giving itself over to the service of the kingdom. Evil is not originated by the ego but has its sources beyond the ego, so that the language of Jesus, referring as it does to Satan and demons, is psychologically quite accurate.

But while the ego is not the originator of evil, it can be taken over by it. And whether or not evil will come to possess the ego may ultimately come down to the matter of sin. The ego is prone to sin, and through sin evil gains a foothold over man. Sin, more than anything else, enables alien powers to possess, distort, and use consciousness, and so cuts man's consciousness off from wholeness and God. So the problem of evil is closely associated with the problem of sin, and it is this to which we must now turn.

Traditionally sin has been identified with the breaking of the laws of God, especially by giving way to passion. The idea is that God has established a body of laws which man is to follow. If he fails to do so—if he infringes on these laws or breaks them—he is sinning. The great prototype for sin is said to be Adam's fall in the Garden of Eden where God told Adam that he must not eat of the fruit of the tree of the knowledge of good and evil, but Adam and Eve disobeyed God, broke His law, and ate the fruit. Thus the original sin is said to be disobedience, and all other sins are likened to it. This attitude toward sin is little different from the legalism of the Pharisees, the only major difference being the substitution of moral prescriptions and ecclesiastical requirements for the Jewish religious legislation. Yet it seems to have escaped the attention of most Christians that in substituting one body of laws for another, Christians have not gone beyond that legalism of the scribes and Pharisees which Jesus condemned so roundly.

The other collective attitude toward sin is that sin

usually involves passion. This is really a variance of the first, since the vast number of the "laws of obedience" which God is said to require of men have to do with the body. Accordingly, the great sins are regarded as sexual sins, including adultery, homosexuality, and masturbation. Even sins of thought are included, as when we have the "wrong" sexual fantasies—perhaps about people one is not "supposed" to be attracted to—or have negative or angry thoughts about people. Since all emotions have their corollary in identifiable chemical processes of the body, this attitude toward sin amounts to a negation of the bodily or natural man. Ecclesiastical imagery has, throughout the ages, populated hell liberally with people who have given way to sins of passion, so that the population of hell in the traditional Christian imagination is made up largely of sexual offenders.

Yet Jesus himself had very little to say about the sins of the flesh. His main concern was with the sins of the spirit, because the sins of the spirit are ten times deadlier than are the sins of the flesh. But somehow it seems to have escaped the attention of traditional Christianity that, in stressing sin as equivalent to the sins of the flesh, we are not following Jesus but are falling prey to a form of Gnosticism, that ancient rival to Christianity which saw the root of evil in the material world and in the body of man, and so split man between his body and his spirit.

In either case the general collective attitude toward sin is: You know better, God gave you the rules, you deliberately chose to flout or ignore them, and now you must be punished. On this idea of sin is based both our penal code and our geography of the hereafter, as a place where punishment for offenders, who have done what we would not let ourselves do, is guaranteed by divine justice. This ethic we can call, in the footsteps of the Russian philosopher Nicholas Berdyaev, the "ethic of obedience."

When we actually look at the Gospels, however, we get a different picture of what constitutes sin. The New Testament word for sin ("amartia" in Greek) means literally to "miss the mark." It is the same word that an archer would use if he shot an arrow at a target and missed it. This seems like a surprisingly benign word to use to describe something as destructive to human life and relationship to God as sin, for, after all, can it be so very bad to miss the mark? But the seriousness of missing the mark is that it reflects back upon the archer. The archer missed the mark because he failed to be on center and shot unconsciously without taking proper aim. There is an illustrative saying of Confucius in which he says that an archer who fails to hit his target must find the fault in himself: "In Archery we have something like the way of the Higher Man. When the archer misses the center of the target he turns around and seeks for the cause of his failure in himself" (Confucius, "Doctrine of the Mean," XIV.5).

The attitude of Jesus toward sin reflects this view that missing the mark has to do with unconsciousness on the part of the individual. According to Jesus' view, sin does not amount to simply breaking the rules of God, but springs from man's unconsciously motivated actions. Sin springs from man's state of moral darkness brought on by a lack of awareness which causes him to "miss the mark." As long as man lives in moral darkness, without knowledge of what he is doing and why, he can only hope to obey a law fixed by God. But such a morality is not a morality of love but of slavish obedience. It is an inferior morality because it is not based upon one's knowledge of oneself and of God but upon an uncreative obedience to regulations imposed from without. There is no love or freedom in a Pharisaic ethic of obedience. Love and freedom can come only through the "ethic of creativity," as Berdyaev calls it. Such an ethic is that of the kingdom of God.

In one ancient manuscript there is a verse immediately following Luke 6:5, and also occurring in early Christian apocryphal literature, which beautifully illustrates this point. According to this saying,

> On the same day, seeing a man working on the sabbath day, he [Jesus] said to him: 'Friend, if you know what you are doing, you are blessed; but if you do not know, you are accursed as a breaker of the Law.'

The point is clear. The Law exists for the regulation of human life. It may be broken only by "those who know what they are doing"; i.e., people who are conscious, who know themselves in depth, including their unconscious motivations. If such a person transcends the Law, *knowing what he is doing*, he is blessed because he has reached a higher, creative ethic. But if he does not know what he is doing, and is acting out of ignorance or self-deception, his sin is a great one.

The key to the ethic of the kingdom of God is, therefore, not obedience but consciousness. Consciousness is usually represented under the symbol of a light, or a lamp, or an eye, something which denotes "seeing"; i.e., psychological knowing. So Jesus says,

'The lamp of the body is the eye. It follows that if your eye is sound, your whole body will be filled with light. But if your eye is diseased, your whole body will be all darkness. If then, the light inside you is darkness, what darkness that will be!' (Matthew 6:22–23/Luke 11:33–36).

The body here is the inner man, and the eye is the organ of spiritual or psychological perception. If our eye, our spiritual insight, is dark, and we are accordingly acting out of ignorance of ourselves, our whole inner life will be dark, for we will in fact be possessed by everything in ourselves of which we are unconscious. But if we are able to act consciously, our whole inner life will be filled with light. This saying of Jesus is sometimes applied to psychosomatic medicine. This is justifiable, for often our body must literally bear the burden of the darkness of our states of mind. But it extends beyond the range of psychosomatic problems to the moral life in general, for the body here can be taken as the equivalent of the inner man or soul.

The stress which the Bible lays upon light and the eye and similar symbols of consciousness is reflected in our dreams. Dream motifs frequently speak of light and darkness. We may be in darkness, struggling to find our way through a dark house, driving down a road without headlights, lost in a dark tunnel, or caught in blackest night. Or we may be blind, or the electric light may fail to turn on, or we may awake in the middle of the night unable to make out a strange figure approaching us. All these images symbolize the difficulty of becoming conscious, and represent the state of psychological darkness under which we are living. On the other hand, we may dream of the sun's

dawning, or of an electric light turning on, or of being high
on a mountain where we can see a long way, or of a flash of
lightning which, like a big insight, illumines a whole landscape. These are symbols of a state of consciousness, of a
"seeing" of the inner reality.

The motif of the eye as a symbol for consciousness is
stressed by Jesus in the following saying:

> 'Why do you observe the splinter in your brother's eye and
> never notice the plank in your own? How dare you say to
> your brother, "Let me take the splinter out of your eye,"
> when all the time there is a plank in your own? Hypocrite!
> Take the plank out of your own eye first, and then you will
> see clearly enough to take the splinter out of your brother's
> eye' (Matthew 7:3–5/Luke 6:41–42).

Clearly the eye here represents consciousness. If our
consciousness is affected by something we do not see and
are not dealing with, we are scarcely in a position to try to
correct our brother. We are in a position to help our
brother only if our own consciousness is clear and in order.
All true morality springs from the clarity of consciousness.
All else is done in darkness and leads to distortions, not to
love.

Now we are in a position to understand Jesus' radical
new ethic with regard to our enemies, an ethic which
forces us to grow in consciousness by seeing even our
enemy as a person and not as a hook on which to hang our
projections:

> 'You have learnt how it was said: You must love your
> neighbor and hate your enemy. But I say this to you: love

your enemies and pray for those who persecute you; in this way you will be sons of your Father in heaven, for he causes his sun to rise on bad men as well as good' (Matthew 5:43/Luke 6:27).

Earlier we noticed how radically different Jesus' attitude toward our enemies is from the collective morality. Collective morality is herd morality, which is a split morality, for it encourages one attitude toward members of our own group and another attitude toward nonmembers. It is fed, as we noted before, by the phenomenon of projection, in which we hate our enemies because we project onto them what we hate in ourselves. As long as our morality does not go beyond this herd morality, we are enslaved and are ruled by an inner darkness. To be sons of the Father, we must go beyond herd morality to individual morality in which we recognize the equality and sanctity of all men before God. Here our feeling of identity comes through our own individuality, and not through our unconsciously having identified with the herd psychology. Such a higher morality is possible only when a person has become conscious, for the unconscious person will remain caught in the herd and will inevitably project onto his enemies what he does not know about himself. Jesus, by calling for a differentiated and conscious attitude toward our enemies as well as our friends, breaks away from collective morality to a morality founded on individual consciousness. It is another example of the creative nature of the ethic of the kingdom of God.

Now we can look again at what Jesus meant when he said, "Except your righteousness shall exceed the righteousness of the scribes and Pharisees, ye shall in no case enter into the kingdom of heaven" (Matthew 5:20 KJV). The Pharisees were experts at following the rules; they were the prize examples of the ethic of obedience. But the ethic of the kingdom requires us to go beyond following the rules to the stage of consciousness where we become aware of our inner opposition and can thus hope to begin to live in light, not in darkness.

We must exceed the righteousness of the scribes and Pharisees by going beyond the Ten Commandments. The Ten Commandments admonish us not to set up the ego as a god in place of God, not to steal, not to commit adultery, not to covet, etc. The ethic of obedience requires only that we meticulously follow these rules. But as we have seen, the Ten Commandments would not be necessary in the first place if there were not someone within us who would do all these things. We have to have the Commandments precisely because we *are* egocentric, we *do* have a thief within us, we *have* adulterous urges, and we *do* covet. The higher morality of the kingdom exceeds the righteousness of following the Law because it leads to a confrontation with the enemy within us who would break these commandments if he had his way. By means of this self-confrontation our whole moral consciousness is lifted to a higher plane. But this requires a differentiated psychological consciousness.

Under the new ethic of the kingdom we can be free from the power of sin, but not free from guilt. This is the paradox of the kingdom. No one can exist as a human being, opposed as he is to himself, without guilt. This inevitable guilt we can call existential guilt, or, in theological language, original sin. But we *can* live free from the power of sin to the extent that we are conscious of our inner opposition. Too many people are so frightened of guilt that they do anything they can to avoid it. They slavishly follow a law, hoping that if they can obey all the Commandments, and always do the "right" thing, they will avoid guilt. The result is a repression of creativity. Nor do we avoid our guilt. Either we believe that we have succeeded in fulfilling all the requirements and are righteous, in which case we are unbearable to everyone else, or we know we are failing and are unbearable to ourselves because we now carry a frightful burden of guilt. The way to the salvation of the kingdom of God is peculiarly paradoxical precisely because it openly acknowledges guilt in order to develop consciousness.

Ellen may be taken as an example. Ellen was raised in a very strict religious household; both her Church and her parents prescribed a rigid following of a Law. Angry thoughts, disobedient impulses, and especially sexual-erotic feelings toward anyone except a husband were strictly of the devil. God was the great Judge and Vigilant Watcher Who recorded one's misdeeds and reserved heaven for the few who could be obedient and hell for the many who would be disobedient. Insecure, afraid of her own impulses, childlike in her adaptation to life, Ellen married a man who himself reflected all these rigid attitudes, and repressed everything within her which would have led to disobedience. But in time the string ran out on this way of life. Her dark side erupted in a violent and uncontrollable anger directed at her husband. Terrified, Ellen sought help as a flood of repressed, forbidden feelings swept over her.

Many months after the first eruption of the unconscious

into consciousness, Ellen fell violently in love with another man. For the first time in her life she experienced powerful erotic feelings, which led her into an affair with this man which she originally experienced as sublime and beautiful. For the time being guilt was ignored in the beauty of the springlike feelings she was experiencing. Later she found that the man she had loved was a fake and a scoundrel. She realized that she had not loved him as a person, because she had not known him as a person, but had simply experienced for the first time the depths of her own eros.

After realizing her mistake in love, her first impulse was to succumb to the judgmental voices within her, her legacy from childhood, which assured her of her eternal damnation for having given way to the worst of all sins. But she was able to see that her brief love affair was a part of the total meaning of her life. She had been wrong and misled in her appraisal of this man. But her feelings themselves, of eros and tenderness, were enormously important. Because these feelings were the motive for her involvement with this man, she was able to integrate her experience. Had she set out deliberately to "flout the law"—had this been her primary motive, and not love—the experience would have been much more difficult to resolve, for the motivation would then have come from the ego, and not from her own inner center. Paradoxically, while she returned to her family, she nevertheless had to have an experience such as this in order to find the depths of herself. She was like the woman who was a sinner in the story of Luke 7:36–50: it was necessary for her to be forgiven much if she was to love much. And it was necessary for her to disobey the

Law and allow herself to be guilty in order to move into consciousness of herself and a higher ethic of creativity.

Evil is separation. Theologically, it is separation from God. Psychologically, it is separation within oneself. The kingdom of God comes to restore unity to man, to unify him with God and with himself. To do this, the mask must be dropped and the "inner enemy" confronted consciously and accepted. Sin is living unconsciously, being under the power of darkness, because without consciousness of self there can be no free choice, only enslavement to what we don't know about ourselves. Only through consciousness can our inner divisions be brought within God's healing power. For this reason the ethic of the kingdom of God requires us to go beyond the ethic of obedience to an ethic of creativity founded upon consciousness. Only with such an ethic can there be freedom, choice, and love.

To do this, we must accept guilt as an inevitable consequence of being human and making choices. For to make choices is to run a risk of being "wrong," and being human is to stop playing it safe and to live life to its fullest. But being guilty is not the equivalent of being under the power of sin and evil. The Law, seeking as it does to free us from guilt, fails to free us from sin and evil. Only the kingdom of God can make us free.

When we acknowledge the inner enemy and experience the birth of a conscious ethic, a connection is established between consciousness and the inner depths. This connection is vitally important, for it is the soul itself. It is to the importance of having a living soul-connection between consciousness and the inner depths to which we now turn.

8

The
Faith of
the Soul

✠✠✠

The word "soul" is
not popular today. Philosophers and scientists often regard
her as a fable, a bit of verbal nonsense. The Church seems
to have little interest in her, although at one time the soul
engrossed the Church deeply. In the mind of the lay person
the soul is likely to be construed as a metaphysical entity
which somehow endures forever through time, and therefore, in today's here-and-now culture, is of no concrete
importance. Yet it is hard to talk of the inner world at all
without speaking of the soul. Somehow the more precise,
clinical language of psychology does not convey the overtones of meaning which adhere to the ancient word "soul."
The soul persists, in spite of all attempts to eradicate it from
our language and thinking.

And well it might. For the plight of modern man is that
he has lost his soul. He is disoriented and sick at heart
because he is out of touch with those things his soul has to
give him. Some suppose that if only all men were materially
well off, all would be well. But this would minister only to
the outer, physical man. The spiritual side of man will

always be in distress as long as the soul is not recognized and loved.

The soul may often appear in our dreams. In the dreams of a man she may appear under the guise of an unusual or beautiful woman whom he greatly loves or yearns for. A woman will also dream of the soul as a woman, sometimes a woman of whom she is jealous, if she is separated from her own eros principle, or possibly a woman whom she admires. The soul may also appear as a bird, a favorite symbol for her since it is a creature which belongs both to the earth and to the sky, and so stands between body and spirit. The bird may be pictured as beautifully colored, or as alighting in our hands, or as soaring into the sky. But if the relationship with the soul is broken, the soul-figure may appear negatively. The woman in our dreams may be angry, or bitter, or ill, or in distress. Or perhaps the beautiful bird has died, or something catastrophic is about to happen as in the following dream which came to Ellen, whose story we discussed previously:

> "I was at a lake where I noticed the most beautiful birds flying in and out of the water. They were in hues of blue, green, and red. Then I saw people kneeling next to the water and clipping the wings of the birds so that they could no longer fly. The birds looked so sad, almost like dead. Agitatedly I asked them why they were doing this. They replied, 'Because they are flying over *our* property, and, therefore, must be punished.' "

Here we see mirrored in the dream the terrible hubris * of the ego which seeks to kill or cripple the soul. The

* An exaggerated development leading to a domineering and prideful inflation.

human ego, inflated with a sense of its own importance, exaggerated in its one-sided development to Luciferian proportions, supposes that it owns and controls Creation, and has a right to clip the wings of the soul herself.

From the point of view of psychology *the soul is that within us which connects a man's consciousness to his inner depths.* The soul's primary function is relationship, and the relationship between the ego and the inner world is the most important relationship of all, for if this is broken, relationships with men and God are impossible. Without the living connection to himself which the soul makes possible, a man is like a ship without a rudder, or like an uprooted tree. Such a man becomes ill, or brutal, or falls into despair, or seeks substitutes in alcohol or drugs.

For a man to have his soul, he must relinquish his identification with his outer mask, and must be willing to face what is within himself. But beyond relinquishing his mask, a person in search of his soul must accept and cherish the principle of *eros,* for the soul, as a function of relatedness, has eros as its primary quality.

Eros is the feminine principle par excellence. Eros is that which binds together, unites, synthesizes, and heals. Eros is the cement of human relationship, the fount of inspiration for social and humanitarian causes, the bond between a man's consciousness and his inner meaning, and the door through which a person walks to spiritual insight. Women naturally lie closer to eros, and therefore to the soul, than do men, which may be one of the reasons why women tend to be more religious and more open to the inner way. But men, too, have a soul within them whose activity is characterized by eros.

Eros, because it gives us the capacity to love, is also the ground of faith. It is out of eros that faith springs, and from faith springs hope, so that a connection to the soul is fundamental to our capacity to affirm life meaningfully and positively. This may be why St. Paul, in speaking of faith, hope, and love, states that "the greatest of these is love" (I Corinthians 13).

Faith is a fundamentally important element in the journey to the kingdom, but the nature of faith has often been misunderstood. When Jesus speaks of faith, he is not thinking of what we might call doctrinal faith. He never asks anyone to believe in any doctrinal, philosophical, or metaphysical creed of any kind. When Jesus speaks of faith, he is speaking of a certain capacity of a person to affirm life in spite of what life may bring, and even in the face of doubts; "Lord, I believe; help thou mine unbelief" (Mark 9:24 KJV). It has little or nothing to do with one's formal, intellectual beliefs, which may actually get in the way of a living faith. It has a great deal to do with the relationship to one's soul, for the soul, with her capacity for love, is in touch with the fundamental meaningfulness of life and so can inspire faith.

Instances of the importance of faith abound in Jesus' sayings (cf. Matthew 8:10/Luke 7:9; Matthew 9:2/Mark 2:5/Luke 5:20; Matthew 9:29; Matthew 15:28; Mark 11:22; Luke 7:50; Luke 8:25/Mark 4:35–41/Matthew 8:23–27). It is fundamental to almost all the healing stories, which characteristically conclude with the words "Thy

faith hath made thee whole" (Matthew 9:22/Mark 5:34/
Mark 10:52/Luke 8:48, 17:19, all KJV). It is also fundamental to the attitude of prayer:

> 'I tell you solemnly, if your faith were the size of a mustard
> seed you could say to this mountain, "Move from here to
> there", and it would move; nothing would be impossible for
> you' (Matthew 17:20/Mark 11:23/Luke 17:6)

and

> 'if you have faith, everything you ask for in prayer you will
> receive' (Matthew 21:22).

Faith, as a grain of mustard seed, is obviously not a
matter of the intellect or will but a function of the soul. A
man in touch with his soul has faith because, like a grain of
mustard seed, he feels his fundamental connectedness to the
wholeness of things. The prayer of faith is a prayer of the
soul, and is efficacious against evil (Matthew 17:19–20;
Luke 22:31–34); it even has power to influence physical
forces of creation. Prayer itself is an activity of the soul
which was also fundamental to Jesus' life and which opens
up the way for the individual to reach the kingdom of
God (Luke 3:21/Luke 5:16/Luke 6:12/Luke 9:18/Luke
11:1/Luke 22:39–41/Matthew 26:36–46/Mark 14:32–
42).

The widespread rejection of faith in our times is part of
our overly intellectualized and rationalized attitude to life.
We are a people who one-sidedly worship the intellect and
reason. We mistake faith for a belief in creedal statements,

or metaphysical doctrines which cannot be proved by science, and so on intellectual grounds we reject it. But if there is little faith today, it is not because it is unscientific —for it is not an intellectual exercise in the first place—but because our one-sided ego development denies the soul, and the denial of the soul denies faith and eros as well. We are a people who value the intellect more than feeling, worldly effectiveness more than personal relatedness, the capacity to make money more than the capacity to heal men. We honor as heroes our scientists, brilliant intellects, and men of war far more than we honor men or women of eros. Even religion today generally denies eros in favor of rationality, obedience to law, and puritanical morality. Or, where these gods are overthrown by the young or avant garde, sexuality is often mistaken for eros and eros is dragged in the mire of hedonism. As a result many women, as well as men, are separated from the eros principle of their souls, and so from their very own selves. Man or woman, the eros side to a person's totality must be accepted, differentiated, and lived if faith is to live and we are to find the kingdom.

Our Lord reflects a living relationship to the soul in both his person and his sayings. In his person his relationship to the soul shows in his enormous personal compassion for people. Jesus was capable of lasting, deep personal relationships, always the mark of a man whose eros side is well developed, and so of a man who is in touch with his soul. This results in a deep compassion for people. So when the crowd has found a woman taken in adultery and is about to stone her, he is able to say,

> 'If there is one of you who has not sinned, let him be the first to throw a stone at her' (John 8:7).

And when he visits Mary and Martha, and Martha chides Mary for not helping in the kitchen but sitting instead at the feet of Jesus to listen to him, Jesus says,

> 'It is Mary who has chosen the better part; it is not to be taken from her' (Luke 10:42).

Poor faithful Martha, driven by her meticulous conscience and forced to fulfill all the "shoulds" and "oughts" of life, is resentful of her sister, who is free of these compulsions. But Mary's soul draws her to Jesus and opens her to the world of the spirit. Jesus himself is sensitive to both persons, uniquely in touch with both of their souls, because he is in touch with his own.

So important is this soul that without it there is nothing of any value in life. Outer things by themselves are not evil, but without the soul they are of no importance. If a man has no soul-connection to himself, his life will come to nothing in the ethic of the kingdom of God. So Jesus says,

> 'For what is a man profited, if he shall gain the whole world, and lose his own soul?' (Matthew 16:26 KJV/Luke 9:25/Mark 8:36).

In typically modern fashion contemporary translations of the New Testament render the word "soul" in this verse as "life." The RSV, for instance, says, "For what will it profit a man, if he gains the whole world and forfeits his life?" (Matthew 16:26). The Jerusalem Bible puts it, "What, then, will a man gain if he wins the whole world and ruins his life?" (Matthew 16:26). We think of our "life" as an outer thing, or our physical existence, or the outer circumstances surrounding us. The soul, however is a psychic reality which makes a man alive from within. In the verse above Jesus is referring to the inner reality of the soul, not to a man's outward life or physical existence, since elsewhere he makes it clear that sometimes one must give up his life in order to find it: "He that loseth his life for my sake shall find it" (Matthew 10:39 KJV). The mere hanging onto physical life, when the time has come to relinquish it, is of no value. But the connection to the soul is of vital importance, for without it our outward life comes to nothing. So also he says,

'Do not be afraid of those who kill the body but cannot kill the soul; fear him rather who can destroy both body and soul in hell' (Matthew 10:28).

Here the allusion is clearly to an inner reality of supreme importance, since the forfeit of our life in the sense of our physical existence is not necessarily fatal to our souls, and may sometimes even be desired, but the destruction of the soul is a calamity.

Since a connection with the soul is a connection to the principle of eros, the place of eros in relationship to the

kingdom must be further explored. Eros springs from nature and carries a feminine sign. It hovers close to the earth
and to the bodily man, and therefore is also close to man's
passions and instincts. This raises the question of the place
of man's bodily nature in the kingdom of God.

The traditional ecclesiastical attitude toward eros and
sexuality has been negative. It is no accident that when
Sigmund Freud peered into the unconscious in the early
part of this century, he saw so much repressed instinctuality that he declared man's basic libido, or drive, to be
sexual-erotic and pleasure-seeking, for centuries of "Christian" repression of the natural side of man had resulted in
an overloading of the unconscious with instinctuality.
There are three reasons why conventional Christianity has
been largely identified with a negative view of the instinctual man and of man's natural feelings.

One reason is the unnatural split between paganism and
Christianity. The usual "Christian" view is that Christianity
is good and paganism is bad, and that there is no connection
between the two. Since man's instinctual, natural feelings
were in existence long before Christianity, and were expressed in pagan mythology and ritual, they took on a
consequently devilish hue. There should be no such split
between the pagan myths and images and the Christian
ones. All myths have their origin in the striving of the
psyche to express in mythological form man's deepest spiritual and psychological truths and strivings. The Christian
image of the God-man, of death and resurrection, of the
miraculous birth of the Saviour, of the divine man who has
healing power and gifts, is not a thing apart from the myths
which existed before the Christian era, but is the outgrowth
and consummation of these myths.

This can be seen, for instance, in the parallel between the story of Jesus' birth and death and the stories of those dying and rising gods of the Eastern Mediterranean which existed in mythology prior to Christ. Adonis, Tammuz, Osiris, Attis, and others have many things in common with Christ. All these pagan deities are closely associated with the Mother; all are gods of healing and salvation; all die an early and untimely death and then rise again; all are worshiped by their followers on their respective "Good Fridays"; the resurrections of all are celebrated with great festivities. They also all die "on the tree"; that is, their death is closely associated with a tree, a wooden casket, or some other symbol of the Great Mother, to whom they are closely tied. But Christ also enjoys a unique relationship to the Mother Goddess, represented in the Virgin Mary; he too is a bestower of healing and blessings; he too dies the early death and rises again, and is worshiped with festivities on Good Friday and Easter; he too dies on the "Tree" of the Cross—in fact, in the first centuries of Christianity the Cross was almost invariably referred to by the Fathers of the Church as "the Tree." It is not hard to see the parallels between pagan myths and the Christian story, which shows that the cleavage between the two is unnatural. Christianity grew out of paganism; it is not a stone thrown from heaven, but the consummation of a living process going on in the psyche of man.

On the other hand, if Christianity grew out of paganism it also goes beyond it. First, because Christianity is not left in the form of a myth but is enacted in history, in the life of a particular person at a particular time. Second, because Christ has a vital relationship not only to the Mother but also to the heavenly Father—an element missing in the dying and rising gods before him. This gives his mission a uniquely spiritual and conscious character, so that for Christ the death on the Cross is not involuntary, as was the case with the others, but is voluntarily chosen, consciously decided upon for a spiritual reason.

So his resurrection is a once-and-for-all event because he partakes of the nature of the heavenly Father, while the resurrections of the others were cyclical, for being only nature gods they died and rose each year. The dying and rising gods of paganism were deities whose death and life followed nature's cycle. Christ also comes from nature, but he is in contact with spirit; and so his resurrection is lineal and not cyclical. All this makes Christianity uniquely different from paganism, and yet it includes the feminine, natural pagan element within it. But the Church has split off this natural element, and in so doing has lost the wholeness inherent in the Incarnation, where, in Christ, nature and spirit became one.

This brings us to our second point. There has long been a great tension between the physical and spiritual sides of man. The instinctual side and the moral side—the bodily man and the intellectual—are in opposition to each other. Christianity allowed the spiritual, moral, conscious side of man to develop as never before. But this side of man is easily overwhelmed by man's instinctuality so that the two seem enemies. Though the Incarnation united the two sides, this union was more than the early Church could maintain. Ancient men were still too close to their instincts, too much in danger of being overwhelmed, so that it was psychologically necessary for them to deny instinct in order that the precariously won world of the spirit might become stronger. But while this denial may at one time have been a psychologically necessary step for man on his road to development, it is no longer appropriate in our age, which must now strive for synthesis.

The third reason for the body-spirit split in man which traditional Christianity has espoused is the ancient struggle in the Church between incarnational Christianity and Gnosticism. The form of paganism which was most dangerous to Christianity was Gnosticism. A complicated religious scheme of salvation with innumerable variations, Gnosticism was a danger to Christianity precisely because in so many respects it resembled it. In fact, many Gnostic teachers began to incorporate Christ into their schemes of salvation when Christianity became influential. This made the Gnostics all the more dangerous, for if it had been permitted, the uniqueness of Christianity would have been lost in the vast, eclectic Gnostic pantheons and speculations.

The Fathers of the Church were aware of this danger. What they objected to most in Gnosticism was its identification of matter with evil, and the rejection of the physical side of man as belonging to the world of the devil. Bravely the early Fathers of the Church spurned this Gnostic attitude toward matter and firmly established the theological basis of incarnational Christianity: that Christ was fully a man, that he had a complete body, that he suffered and died a physical death, that God created the material world, and that it was good.

But having won the battle theologically against the Gnostics, the Church lost it psychologically by continuing to preach an *ethic* which, in effect, labeled the bodily side of man as evil after all. This was the ethic of asceticism, which denied the body in favor of the spirit and virtually identified passion with sin. So in the end the Church became partially Gnostic after all, and, in their attitudes toward sin and the natural side of man, many "Christians" today are, in fact, Gnostics.

But in Jesus there is no asceticism or Gnosticism, no devaluation of the body, no separation from nature. To the contrary he was accused by the Pharisees of being a "wine drinker and a glutton." The sins Jesus attacked were not sins of the flesh. Man should not use his body sinfully, to be sure, but the most dangerous sins were those of the spirit. Hypocrisy, deceit, self-righteousness, allying oneself with Satan—these were the truly deadly sins; they were far more dangerous to the soul than were the excesses of the body. There is not one single phrase from the lips of Jesus in condemnation of the instinctual side of man. To the contrary, his language is full of the imagery of nature; he loved the things of the earth and used earthy images to express the divine essence.

If Jesus was not married, it was not because he was averse to sexuality or to women, but because he was conscious of a unique mission he was to perform which precluded marriage, and also because he carried his marriage *on the inside*. His marriage was the marriage from within, the union of masculine and feminine within himself, as we shall see in more detail later on. Rather than being opposed to the feminine side of life, he was in close contact with women throughout his ministry. This is especially surprising since in his day it was forbidden for a man to have social contact with women. Yet Jesus numbered women among his closest friends; they responded to him with deep love and gratitude; they stood by him at the Cross and were the first at the empty tomb.

As soon as we get into the unconscious, we know that Jesus was right in not denying the natural side of man. Man is a totality of body, soul, and spirit. He is not any one of these things, but all three together in a mystical unity. If any one side of man is denied, it imperils the full expression of the other. So if people deny that they have aggressive feelings, they will also deny their sexual feelings; and if the sexual feelings cannot be consciously acknowledged, it becomes impossible to fulfill eros. But if eros is stifled, spirituality is also stifled and becomes rigid, hard, judgmental, and uncreative. Man's totality is organic. If any one part of man's being suffers, the total human organism suffers. If the total man is to live, to be free, to come into expression, all sides of man must be consciously recognized and joyfully received as given by God.

While the instinctual life and emotions are to become conscious, they are not to dominate any more than spirit is to dominate. If all impulses toward pleasure and all sensual or erotic feelings are gratified without regard to other values, this is done at the expense of man's spiritual nature. The liberation of the natural man is not a liberation to license but to consciousness. To act only on the pleasure principle is to deny both eros, which seeks relationship as well as gratification, and spirit, which seeks for meaning and completeness. The ethic of the kingdom requires that *all* sides of man's nature are to become conscious, but no one side is to predominate at the expense of the other.

Our modern era tends to forget this. It has supposed that it could liberate instinct by giving it license, but this has been done at the expense of relatedness to others and to spirit. The result has not been wholeness or health, but another form of neurosis and sickness as troublesome as that which results from the repression of instinct.

An all too typical case from my pastoral experience illustrates the point. A young man and woman decide to live together without benefit of marriage; then justify this on the basis that sexual feelings are to be freed from conventional restraint. All this time the young man knows that he does not love the girl, and corresponds with another girl whom he hopes to marry. The young woman with whom he is sleeping, meanwhile, tries her very best to get pregnant. Neither loves the other, romantically or as a human being. The young man uses the woman as an object, a body through which to gratify himself; he finds pleasure through using her and satisfies his doubts about his masculinity. The young woman also uses him. She hopes to get pregnant to force a marriage which is against his will, and is willing to prostitute herself to him rather than face the anxiety of being without a man. The arrangement is not free love, but free sex, for there is no love in it. It results in a destruction of eros, for there is only manipulation in the relationship, not eros. It is a dehumanizing relationship to both because each uses the other. And spirit is denied absolutely, for neither partner scrutinizes his or her behavior in the light of any value system other than egocentric goals. But the sin in all this is not sex as such, but the unconsciousness of two people which leaves them victims of their egocentricity.

How can there be a way out of such a dilemma? The way of the kingdom is to unite the opposites within man, and thereby find God. *By being perfectly conscious of all that is within us, accepting and feeling the fire of all our emotions, but containing this fire in the crucible of our total personality, a process of unification and transformation can take place in which we are lifted to a higher level of being.* But to do this, we will have to have a higher value to which instinct must submit. This is why Jesus says,

'You have learnt how it was said: You must not commit adultery. But I say this to you: if a man looks at a woman lustfully, he has already committed adultery with her in his heart' (Matthew 5:27–28).

To look at a woman lustfully is to desire to have her only for the purpose of pleasurable gratification. This turns the personality of the woman into an object, a thing to be used for egocentric satisfaction. It is a depersonalization of the woman and hence also depersonalizes us. Where lust is gratified, it is at the expense of eros, which calls for personal relatedness, and of spirit, which subordinates all to a higher meaning. A man who looks at a beautiful woman and denies that he could have sexual fantasies about her is either lying or out of touch with his instinctual life. Almost any man would be able to find physical pleasure experiencing sex with a desirable woman as a partner. But the man who would belong to the kingdom of God does not allow his sexuality to become lust, for in so doing his instinctuality, by excluding eros and spirit, would become a part dominating the whole and hence would serve evil.

The ethic of the kingdom of God calls for sexuality to be

conscious but not expressed unless the expression affirms
the principles of eros and spirit as well. This explains the
otherwise enigmatic saying of Jesus concerning eunuchs.
After discussing divorce, Jesus says,

> 'It is not everyone who can accept what I have said, but only
> those to whom it is granted. There are eunuchs born that
> way from their mother's womb, there are eunuchs made so
> by men and there are eunuchs who have made themselves
> that way for the sake of the kingdom of heaven. Let anyone
> accept this who can' (Matthew 19:11–12).

One who has become a eunuch for the sake of the kingdom of heaven has sacrificed the direct, physical expression
of his sexuality in order to consummate a higher union of
the opposites within himself. While conscious of and accepting his sexual feelings, he does not allow their direct
gratification. Nor is the great eros he may feel allowed
consummation in a sexual relationship with the beloved,
even though the feelings of eros are not repressed but are
being made conscious. The result of containing the fire
within oneself is an inner development, the generation of
the inner marriage which is the equivalent of the kingdom
of God.

This was the reason Plato prescribed "Platonic love" in
his dialogues "Phaedo" and "Symposium." Platonic love is
not a love devoid of emotion or sexual feelings. To the
contrary, Plato makes it perfectly clear that such a love is
intense and filled with desire. But by refusing to concretize
the love in a sexual relationship, says Plato, the god Eros is
introduced. Eros then leads the lover into communion with

the realm of Ideas, and the whole development of that person is uplifted.

This is also the reason the early Church so often prescribed chastity. Only later was this part of a polemic against sex; at first it was to prepare the soul to receive Christ as the bridegroom. Instead of concretizing love on the outside in a sexual relationship, a person's love was to be so conscious but contained that it would prepare the soul to receive the heavenly bridegroom. The inner marriage was thus achieved in lieu of the outer marriage.

By being conscious of eros and sexuality, but not allowing these feelings illicit concrete expression, we shall find it possible to relate to that image of the union of opposites which is the archetypal image underlying all sexuality and all eros relationships. As we will see in Chapter 10, the great image par excellence by which the kingdom is expressed is the image of the heavenly marriage. It is this central image, the most powerful of all man's psychic symbols, which constellates the sexual feelings and fantasies. As long as we live for easy gratification of the feelings aroused by this image, we never achieve the inner unification, the totality to which the image calls us, for then we are trying to realize the totality in an unconscious and unindividual way on the outside, rather than consciously on the inside.

The ethic of the kingdom is an ethic of consciousness. To achieve the kingdom, nothing that belongs to us must be denied conscious recognition and acceptance as a genuine part of our totality. Sexuality and eros, too long excluded from consciousness by a Gnosticizing Church, must also be allowed conscious recognition. In this way the connection with the soul is maintained, for as long as we are seeking consciousness we keep our soul, but if we renounce consciousness and reject what belongs to us, banishing it into darkness, we lose our soul. With the connection with the soul, the whole of ourselves may begin to come into conscious expression. The movement now is toward synthesis, toward a union of the personality in depth. Necessarily, parts of ourselves long overlooked, long banished to the darkness of our inner hells, will come to the surface. What once was lost in us will now be found, and this will be an event of supreme importance.

9

The
Lost Coin

✤✤✤

With the relationship
of consciousness to the soul, the whole inner world is now
available for recognition and integration. The process of
the establishment of the kingdom in the life of an individual
involves the inclusion of what was hitherto unrecognized
and unknown. This is by no means always a pleasant or an
enjoyable experience, since much of what must be included
appears at first to be objectionable, inferior, or unwanted,
and consequently even devilish. Yet without these "lost"
aspects of ourselves, the "perfection"—i.e., wholeness—of
the kingdom cannot be established, for they constitute our
unredeemed humanity which must now be found.

It is inevitable that, in the growth of our personalities,
much that potentially is part of us will not be developed.
Our early identification with the mask effectively excludes
a large portion of our total personality. Our identification
with our masculinity, if we are men, or femininity, if we
are women, will also exclude much of our potential. We
also know that the ego, in order to be able to function
effectively in the world and cope with life, will cultivate
those psychological functions which it can use to maximum

advantage at the expense of others.* At first such one-sidedness is necessary if the ego is to get into life; but later
what was once a useful adaptation blocks the way, for a
one-sided development leaves too much of the total personality undeveloped and in the chaos of the unconscious. All
this undeveloped self is the "unlived life," which, for the
kingdom to be realized, must get out into life in a legitimate
way.

The undeveloped side of our personality will appear in
our dreams. It may be seen under the guise of the beggar
who comes to our door, or perhaps of an inferior man or
woman, or of a crippled or handicapped person, or of a
child who has not yet developed. The need to reclaim this
part of ourselves may be mirrored in a dream of a great
descent, or in a dream figure who cries for help, or a scene
which resembles the world of hell, for hell is the abode of
all that is within us which is separated from consciousness
and denied access to life.

The unlived life may also sometimes seize the initiative
and make a great bid for freedom, in which case there is a
turbulence of personality, a violent inner upheaval as the
unused portions of ourselves stage a revolt. If we identify
with the rebellion, this will be a frightening experience to
those around us. Husband or wife, parents, or peers may be
alarmed at the sudden changes which they see taking place.
If we are not identified with the surging forces, the fear
will be our own, for such a person is deeply frightened of
himself, may even fear insanity, or feel forced to quell the
rebellion by taking refuge in drugs or some other form of

* See the discussion of the four functions, page 28 in Chapter 1.

psychological escapism. The rebellion of the lost parts of the psyche may also take place socially, in which case there is a time of great social unrest as people are stirred collectively by forces from within of which they are only dimly aware. Such a social upheaval is unquestionably taking place today, as long-repressed "Dionysus" seeks to break out. Earthquakes, wars, revolts, floods—all are typical dream images which have to do with the clamor from within for the inclusion of what has hitherto been rejected and denied.

⊕

There are a great many sayings of Jesus which speak of the need to reclaim what has been denied in order that the kingdom might be complete. So Jesus says,

'the Son of Man has come to seek out and save what was lost' (Luke 19:10).

In its missionary zeal Christianity has usually taken this to mean that Christ came to save those people "out there" who are lost. In ancient times this might have referred to the Gentiles; in modern times it has been taken to mean anyone—from the slum dweller to the native of the darkest Amazon—who was supposed to be "lost" because he was not yet Christianized. No doubt there *is* an outer significance to this saying of Jesus, and he did come to save all persons, wherever they are, who are lost to God. But the reference is also internal. He came as the Son of Man, as the archetype of human completeness, to seek out and save all those parts of man's personality, wherever they exist, which are lost to consciousness. The act of redemption is not only outer and social; it is also inner and psychological.

> 'When you give a lunch or a dinner, do not ask your friends, brothers, relations or rich neighbours, for fear they repay your courtesy by inviting you in return. No; when you have a party, invite the poor, the crippled, the lame, the blind; that they cannot pay you back means that you are fortunate, because repayment will be made to you when the virtuous rise again' (Luke 14:12–14).

Here is another of the many sayings of Jesus which refer to both the social and the psychological attitude the Christian is to cultivate. Socially he is to include in his circle of concern the unfortunate people around him. Psychologically he is to do the same, by including those parts of himself which have hitherto been denied development. At first this seems futile, as though we must accept in us what is unacceptable, useless, or actually defeating to our conscious purposes. Where is our reward in this? But when the kingdom comes, when "the virtuous rise," we shall be amply repaid, for we shall have paved the way for totality.

There are also many parables which speak of the necessity of including the inferior element. One of these is the Parable of Lazarus and the Rich Man (Luke 16:19–31). There was a rich man who had everything his way in life, and a beggar named Lazarus who had nothing and used to long just for the scraps that fell from the rich man's table. When both died, the rich man went to Hades, where he was in torment, but Lazarus went to the bosom of Abraham. The rich man appealed to Abraham to send Lazarus to him to cool his tongue with water and ease his agony in the flames. But Abraham replied that not only was it fitting that the rich man should have this experience, the reverse of the situation he had on earth, but in addition there was now a great gulf fixed between the two so that Lazarus could not cross over even if he wished. The rich man appealed to Abraham to have Lazarus sent to his five brothers to urge them to repent before it is too late. Abraham said, "They have Moses and the prophets." The rich man urged that this was not enough, but that if one came to them from the dead they would repent. To which Abraham answered,

'If they will not listen either to Moses or to the prophets, they will not be convinced even if someone should rise from the dead.'

On the surface this looks like the kind of story the early Church might have encouraged, or perhaps even invented, to put in their place Jews who refused to believe in the Resurrection. But if it is taken inwardly, the rich man is the ego, who has everything its own way and falls prey to a hubris—that is, an inflated idea of its own importance—so that it unfairly dominates the entire psyche. The poor man, Lazarus, is the rejected one, a personality shoved by the ego into the unconscious where it longs for acceptance and for nourishment from consciousness but is denied it. When such a condition persists, the result is an eventual reversal of things. Sooner or later such an ego is plunged into the hell-fire of the unconscious; only in this way can the hubris be overcome, as is seen in the case of King Nebuchadnezzar (Daniel, Chapter 4). This is why Abraham was quite right in pointing out that the brothers of the man would not repent no matter who came to them. Repentance for an ego possessed by an inflated idea of its importance is possible only through being plunged into the fires of the unconscious, fires which have been fed by all the rejected psychic material of the personality. The "inferior personality"—that is, Lazarus in the story—is, on the other hand, elevated by God. The story shows that what man has regarded as inferior, unworthy, and to be scorned is favored, loved, and elevated by God.

As far as this story goes, there is no redemption. A great gulf has now been fixed between the rich man in hell and Lazarus in Abraham's bosom. The great gulf, of course, has been established by the ego itself. It is the inevitable result of the refusal of the ego to acknowledge inner reality; now the ego must suffer the consequences of the great gulf in order to become conscious of the total psyche. In Christian terms, redemption of this situation is possible only by the Christ, who himself descends into hell and so bridges the gulf. Psychologically, the meaning of the doctrine of the descent into hell is a way of saying that, in spite of the gulf the ego makes within the psyche and the creation of an inner hell, Christ can overcome the gulf by descending into all parts of our being.

Two other parables concerned with the motif of the recovery of the lost or inferior parts of the personality are the Parables of the Lost Sheep and the Lost Coin.

'Tell me. Suppose a man has a hundred sheep and one of them strays; will he not leave the ninety-nine on the hillside and go in search of the stray? I tell you solemnly, if he finds it, it gives him more joy than do the ninety-nine that did not stray at all' (Matthew 18:12–14/Luke 15:4–7).

It is interesting that there is a total of precisely one hundred sheep. Jesus might have said, "Suppose a shepherd lost a sheep," or, "Suppose a man had a large herd of sheep." The specific use of the number 100 is part of the parable, and, like all the numbers in the New Testament, has an inner meaning; for numbers, for the early Christians, all had a mystical—or, as we would say today, psychological—significance. The five brothers in the story of Lazarus may refer to the number for humanness, since we have five senses and five extremities to the body. The number 5 is often associated with the physical or natural man. Similarly, Christ's body bears five wounds.

St. Augustine says, "We must not despise the science of numbers, which in many passages of holy Scripture, is found to be of eminent service to the careful interpreter." * He goes on to say that all heathen studies must be rejected, except "the sciences of reasoning and of number," and by the science of number he includes both the ordinary mathematical properties of numbers and their mystical meaning.† The importance of the meaning of numbers for Biblical interpretation is so great that he declares, "Ignorance of numbers prevents us from understanding things that are set down in Scripture in figurative and mystical ways." In all of this, Augustine's attitude is typical of the generally mystical, psychological attitude of early Christianity. We could ignore all this as superstition and reject the idea that Jesus

* *The City of God*, XI.xxx.
† *On Christian Doctrine*, II.39.

had in mind anything mystical when he used numbers, except that numbers recur in our dreams with peculiarly characteristic meanings. As in this parable, so in our dreams there is frequently an emphasis on *the number*. We are in the company of precisely four people, or are handed a bill for exactly $500, or observe in our dreams that it is eight o'clock in the morning. In such a case the dream, through the use of numbers, is insisting on a particular archetypal meaning.

In the early Church the number 10, with its multiples of 100 or 1000, was the divine number. As the total of the four primary numbers 1, 2, 3 and 4, it was the number for unity, but unlike 1, which represented unity on a simple level, the 10, or square or cube of 10, represented unity on a complex level: the many united into one. So it was the number for totality, or God. Methodius writes, "For a thousand, consisting of a hundred multiplied by ten, embraces a full and perfect number" (*Banquet of the Ten Virgins*, Chapter xi). *This is why the loss of just one sheep is so extremely important.* The one lost sheep must be found or the one hundred will not be complete; one might as well end up with thirty-seven or forty-five as with ninety-nine as far as completeness is concerned. This also explains the great joy over having found the one lost sheep. The recovery of what was lost is as important as retaining the ninety-nine because it is essential to the complete number.

Psychologically, the one lost sheep represents the lost part of ourselves, the part of our total personality which is submerged in the depths, caught in the hell of our inner separation, and which must be recognized and brought into expression if we are to be complete. A similar motif is found in the Parable of the Lost Coin.

'Or again, what woman with ten drachmas would not, if she lost one, light a lamp and sweep out the house and search thoroughly till she found it? And then, when she had found it, call together her friends and neighbours? "Rejoice with me," she would say "I have found the drachma I lost"' (Luke 15:8–9).

Now a drachma is worth about six cents, so it is not a very valuable coin. Yet the woman who has lost this coin goes to great efforts to find it and then has a celebration when it is recovered. One explanation, offered by K. C. Pillai, is that in the Orient a woman was given ten coins by her husband at the time of their betrothal as a pledge of love and loyalty. These coins she was to retain all her life. If she was so careless as to lose them, it was a terrible disgrace and an ominous portent for the marriage. This would explain why the woman went to such lengths to find the lost coin and why she called together her friends to celebrate her recovery of the lost piece. We see here again the symbolism of the 10. The missing coin is necessary if there is to be completeness. As far as their symbolic value is concerned, one might as well lose eight or nine of the coins as to lose one of them.

The lost coin is, again, the lost part of ourselves, the inferior part which must be recovered if we are to be complete. Notice also that the woman "lights a lamp." To find what is missing in ourselves requires an act of consciousness, the lighting of the lamp of our mind, and then a thorough searching of our souls, a sweeping out of the inner world.

The inner meaning of these parables did not escape the early Church Fathers. Gregory of Nyssa says, in reference to the lost sheep, that it represents "our lost humanity" (*Against Eunomius*, Book XII). Of the lost coin, he writes that the woman is the soul itself and that the candle which is lighted signifies "doubtless our reason which throws light on hidden principles" (i.e., consciousness which perceives the hidden unconscious). The coin, he notes, is to be found "in one's own house, that is, within oneself." He then goes on to make a most interesting observation concerning the lost coin: "by that coin the Parable doubtless hints at the image of our King, not yet hopelessly lost, but hidden beneath the dirt." This dirt "is the impurity of our flesh, which, being swept and purged away by carefulness of life, leaves clear to the view the object of our search. . . . Verily, all those powers which are the housemates of the soul, and which the Parable names her neighbors for this occasion, when so be that the image of the mighty King is revealed in all its brightness at last, that image which the fashioner of each individual heart of us has stamped upon this our Drachma, will then be converted to that divine delight and festivity, and will gaze upon *the ineffable beauty of the recovered one*" (*On Virginity*, Chapter XII; italics mine).

Here we have the mystery that to recover the lost coin within ourselves—our own unredeemed humanity—is to recover Christ the King himself, the psychological equivalent of which is totality. He is hidden in the depths of the unconscious, where he is both the savior and the one to be saved. He comes in dirt and mire and in all that is objectionable; but when he is recovered to consciousness, we gaze upon ineffable beauty!

A similar motif is struck in the following words of Jesus:

> 'I was hungry and you gave me food; I was thirsty and you gave me drink; I was a stranger and you made me welcome; naked and you clothed me, sick and you visited me, in prison and you came to see me. . . . I tell you solemnly, in so far as you did this to one of the least of these brothers of mine, you did it to me' (Matthew 25:35–36, 40).

These are clearly among the great verses on which the social message of Christianity is founded. We are to minister to our brother in need and, in so doing, we minister also to Christ. But Gregory of Nyssa's reflections make it clear that this passage is also to be taken inwardly. There is a stranger in us—a naked, needy, hungry portion of ourselves, a lost brother of our own soul—and he is also to be reclaimed by being accepted consciously and allowed expression in life. *In so doing, we bring Christ into our lives.* Christ himself is in that lost part of our souls, for by including "the lost coin" we constellate our wholeness.

Phil is a gifted professional person. He was accustomed to success, and with his well-developed mind and skills and high professional standing it was easy for him to fall prey to an inflation which was fed by his wife, who consistently molded herself to try to fit into his opinions. Phil became judgmental, rigid in his attitudes, looking down on others as inferior if their ideas did not fit into his own. He put his wife into a "box," and made her life conform to his by fashioning a marriage which appeared more like a strait jacket than a true union. In fact, however, he was emotionally very dependent on his feeling, intuitive wife, which he painfully realized when she eventually revolted and, casting aside her fears, decided to leave the marriage.

Phil's house of cards began to fall apart. He experienced emotions and anxieties so disturbing in himself that his outer façade could no longer hold together. He was at last driven to seek help for himself and to achieve painful insights which led him to see that his assumed superiority was only a covering for his deep inner needs. As long as he was forcing all his feelings into a box, he was also forced to contain his feeling-type wife in a boxed-in relationship. Gradually, as he became freer, he was able to let his wife become free, so that she no longer felt compelled to leave him. The experience for him was painful, even humiliating at times, but he was becoming whole. His "Lazarus" was being recognized, accepted, fed, given a place in his house, and as a result the gulf within himself was being healed.

Phil's future looks brighter than ever now. As a professional person he is becoming more understanding and nonjudgmental of his clients while not losing any of his skills. But it took a bitter experience and a time of great hurt and confusion to bring him to this point.

This characteristic stage of arriving at the kingdom of God is beautifully portrayed in the famous Parable of the Good Samaritan.* Most of us are so familiar with this story that our awareness of its profound inner meaning has dimmed. We know the story: that a man journeys to Jericho, falls among thieves, is left for dead, and is ignored by

---

* I want to thank Miss Margaret Brown of San Diego for her helpful insights into this parable.

the priests and Levites. Only the despised Samaritan stops to help him, ministers to him, and provides for his continued recovery at a nearby inn. From the outer point of view Jesus is teaching us the kind of attitude we should have toward others. We should be like the Samaritan, able to act from kindness and generosity toward others even if they are not of our own group or kind.

This is perfectly legitimate and true as far as it goes. But, looking at the parable inwardly, we find our identity not in the Samaritan, but in the man who fell among thieves. Phil, for instance, was a man who "fell among thieves." While on his journey through life, he fell prey to his own collective, rigid attitudes, which in a time of crisis left him bleeding and beaten on the road. In this crisis all that was respectable and accepted—the priests and Levites—passed him by. These persons in his life whom he had most adulated, and whose acceptance he most wanted, were the very ones whose opinions he feared in his time of crisis. Nor could he turn for help to his own collective values, for there was no mercy in them, only expedience and "respectability."

Salvation comes from the "Samaritan." The Samaritan is the despised one, the one in ourselves whom we have looked down upon for so long. In Phil's case the inclusion of all the feelings and yearnings he dreaded most in himself actually came to his rescue. In being ministered to by his inferior side, he found his heart and feelings again and could make a beginning toward wholeness.

But in order to find this salvation, Phil had to sacrifice a great deal. Previously he had relied upon logic, rationality, and a rigid ego. In the time of crisis these were of no avail. He had to give up, temporarily, the very ego attitudes which had been the pillars of his personality up to that time, and sacrifice rationality in order to let in the irrationality of the inner world. He had to relinquish thinking attitudes in order to feel what his heart had to tell him, and surrender a reliance on will power in order to come into relationship with the soul.

The paradox of the kingdom is that the very things in life which hitherto have given us such support may now have to be sacrificed. So Jesus says,

> 'If your right eye should cause you to sin, tear it out and throw it away; for it will do you less harm to lose one part of you than to have your whole body thrown into hell. And if your right hand should cause you to sin, cut it off and throw it away; for it will do you less harm to lose one part of you than to have your whole body go to hell' (Matthew 5:29–30).

To take this saying outwardly and literally would be an absurdity. But it makes perfect sense if we take it inwardly and psychologically. The "right" side represents the side of ourselves which is consciously developed, while the "left" side is the side of ourselves of which we are unconscious, since, while our right hand does what we will it to, the left hand for most people seems clumsy and perverse. If we look at it this way, the meaning of Jesus' saying is quite clear: We must at times sacrifice exactly what has been psychologically developed if it so takes over that it excludes our totality. Phil had to sacrifice his "right eye" and "right hand," but by so doing his "whole body" was saved from hell.

This brings us to the final paradox of the Lost Coin. At

first it looks as though consciousness, from its superior development and vantage point, must stoop down to lift up the inner beggar, to rescue the undeveloped inner man, or to go in search of the lost sheep. But at the same time it is the lost part of ourselves, the despised one, the Samaritan, who rescues us. *Our conscious life, cut off from the totality of its own being, stands in need of redemption, so that the despised "inner beggar" side of ourselves appears at the end as the Savior.* We are saved when the lost part of the personality is recovered, for this brings with it the King, the total man, the One in us who brings us joyfully into the kingdom of God. This mystery of the secret identity between Savior and despised one was known to Isaiah, who was able to say of the future Christ that he was

a thing despised and rejected by men,
a man of sorrows and familiar with suffering,
a man to make people screen their faces;
he was despised and we took no account of him.

(Isaiah 53:3)

With the removal of the hubris of the ego, and the inclusion of the inferior, hitherto unconscious parts of our personality which our connection to the soul has made possible, we are now in a position to receive the kingdom of God. What it means for the kingdom to enter into our consciousness, or more exactly, what it means for us to enter into the kingdom, is the subject to which we now turn.

10

The
Coming of
the Kingdom

✠✠✠

With the inclusion of what was once rejected by consciousness, the kingdom can be established as our inner center. This is at once a surrender of the ego to the supremacy of the kingdom and the fulfillment of the ego and its establishment in a position of strength and importance as the representative of the totality of the personality. So Jesus tells us,

> 'Anyone who finds his life will lose it; anyone who loses his life for my sake will find it' (Matthew 10:39/Luke 9:24/Mark 8:35)

and

> 'Anyone who exalts himself will be humbled, and anyone who humbles himself will be exalted' (Matthew 23:12/Luke 14:11).

The sayings apply both outwardly and inwardly. Outwardly this is the call by Christ to a life marked by commitment, not by self-seeking. But this is possible only if the same event has occurred inwardly and the ego has sacrificed its egocentricity to the larger life within.

This must not be confused with weakness. This is not a call to extinguish, nullify, or devalue the ego. The position of the ego in the total personality is one of extreme importance. There can be no wholeness, no strength, no capacity to be used by God without a strong ego. It is only an ego made strong by inner confrontation which is capable of performing the act of self-sacrifice. A weak ego feels compelled to fight and struggle for its very existence. Out of fear the weak ego will defend itself against life and the inner world by means of an assortment of egocentric defenses and attitudes which prevent it from turning itself over to be used by the kingdom.

We cannot sacrifice what we do not have. A person not in possession of himself cannot turn himself over to God for His use. The call is to greater—not less—ego strength, in the psychological sense. Such a person will not be proud but humble, for self-pride can be dispensed with by a strong person. Take the case of Moses, who certainly was a strong person, yet of whom it was said at the end of his life, "Now Moses was the most humble of men, the humblest man on earth" (Numbers 12:3). So Jesus says,

'Blessed are the poor in spirit: for theirs is the kingdom of heaven' (Matthew 5:3 KJV/Luke 6:20).

The Greek word for "poor" means literally "beggarly." The "poor in spirit" are those who recognize that they must beg for their spirit from a source beyond themselves. Such people find the kingdom, while those who regard themselves as self-sufficient do not receive the highest gift.

The giving up of the ego does not come readily to men, whose natural, unconscious inclination is to seek power for themselves and to try to exploit life for their own purposes. The very idea of turning the ego over to a higher power from within produces anxiety because it *looks* as though this means that the ego will be extinguished. In fact, the old ego does die in order that a new ego may be born, and this is the heart of the Christian mystery of transformation. Now we are in a position to see exactly why Jesus said,

> 'Enter by the narrow gate, since the road that leads to perdition is wide and spacious, and many take it; but it is a narrow gate and a hard road that leads to life, and only a few find it' (Matthew 7:13–14/Luke 13:24).

For the narrow way is the anxious way, and the anxious way occurs when the ego must give place to the kingdom.

This giving way of the ego to the greater reality within is often shown in our dreams as a death. We may dream of dying, or of having a mortal illness, or of finding ourselves under sentence of death. The death of the ego in our dreams expresses the necessity for the "death" of the old conscious orientation in order that a new personality, oriented to the inner kingdom, may come. When this inner process is denied, it may lead to compulsive, obsessive thoughts about dying—an irrational conviction, with no physical evidence for it, that we have cancer or some other deadly disease. Actual physical death is suggested in our dreams in another way, and the death of the ego in dreams can almost always be taken as symbolic of a psychological process.

The new personality, which acknowledges that there is a greater reality, is pictured by Jesus as a little child, for it has psychologically only recently been born.

> At this time the disciples came to Jesus and said, 'Who is the greatest in the kingdom of heaven?' So he called a little child to him and set the child in front of them. Then he said, 'I tell you solemnly, unless you change and become like little children you will never enter the kingdom of heaven. And so, the one who makes himself as little as this little child is the greatest in the kingdom of heaven' (Matthew 18:1–4/Luke 9:46–48/Mark 9:33–37).

The child is frequently used by Jesus to represent one who has entered the kingdom of heaven. Earlier we saw that one reason for this is that the little child has no mask; he is what he seems to be and expresses directly what he feels without hypocrisy. But the other reason the child is the prototype of the kingdom of heaven is that the child has a free connection to the inner world. The disciples came to Jesus with an ego attitude: "Who is the greatest in the kingdom of heaven?" This is the ego's ancient desire to "puff itself up." As long as the ego is seeking the kingdom of heaven only to exploit it for its own purposes, it cannot enter. One must enter as a little child: with no false façade, newborn, and closely connected to the inner world, from which spring imagination, spontaneity, and creativity.

This image of the child is the reverse of childishness. We all have a child-self within us. Partly a remnant of our own childhood psyche, partly archetypal in nature, the child-self is an important part of our psychology. If we deny the child within us, we become childish. We do not free ourselves from the child within by denying him, but fall victim to his negative qualities in the form of infantile, regressive, or dependent attitudes. But if we recognize and accept the legitimacy of the child-self, so that we become as a little child in the positive sense, then the child-self is expressed in our personality as freedom, creativity, and the continual generation within us of new life.

For this reason the appearance of the child within our dreams is always of importance. A child may appear who is forlorn, orphaned, neglected, or crippled in some way; in this way the dream calls our attention to the need to recognize and accept the child-self. Or the child may be a happy companion to us, or may take us by the hand, or may be seen at play, thus representing inner creativity. The dream may show the birth of a child, a newborn infant who represents a new life within. Or there may be one or a group of mischievous boys, showing creative elements within us which are likely to be disturbing to the *status quo* of consciousness, but which are valuable for the future growth of the personality. The child may even symbolize the kingdom itself, as Isaiah sensed,

> The wolf lives with the lamb,
> the panther lies down with the kid,
> calf and lion cub feed together
> *with a little boy* to lead them.
> The cow and the bear make friends,
> their young lie down together.
> The lion eats straw like the ox.

The infant plays over the cobra's hole;
into the viper's lair
the young child puts his hand.
(Isaiah 11:6–8; italics mine)

With the relinquishing of egocentricity and the relatedness of the ego to the contents of the inner world, the
kingdom may be established as a center of unity within the
personality. Ordinarily our personality is fragmented because it is split up into pairs of opposites which are hostile
and antagonistic. This is expressed in dreams in which there
is a motif of war, violence, enmity, or opposition in one
form or another. The kingdom comes as a unity—a paradoxical unity since it is a union of factors which are different from each other, and so have a natural inclination to
opposition. *For this reason the most important single image
of the kingdom is the image of the wedding,* since here opposing elements are united. In Jesus' Parable of the Wedding Feast (Matthew 22:2–14/Luke 14:15–24), we have
already noted this motif:

'The kingdom of heaven may be compared to a king who
gave a feast for his son's wedding' (Matthew 22:2).

Outwardly, the king may be likened to God as the Father, and the son likened to Christ, while those who would
not come are the Jews who were originally the chosen
people but would not accept the Lord. This interpretation
is allegorical and not particularly morally edifying. The
deeper meaning is its inner significance. God is the king,
and the wedding to which we are called is the inner wedding, the union of the opposites within us. The ego must

also participate in the inner process and so is summoned to the feast; it is a thing of honor and joy that we should be so called. But the great bulk of humanity is too concerned with outward things to appreciate the value of the inner realm. Only those forced by God to come in, *good and bad alike*, join the wedding feast.

Another wedding parable is the Parable of the Ten Bridesmaids.

'The kingdom of heaven will be like this: Ten bridesmaids took their lamps and went to meet the bridegroom' (Matthew 25:1).

Of these ten bridesmaids five are prepared; their lamps are trimmed and stocked with oil. The other five are unprepared, so that when the bridegroom arrives they have to hurry out to get oil. By the time they do this it is too late; the others are already in the wedding hall and the door is closed. The parable concludes with Jesus' words,

'So stay awake, because you do not know either the day or the hour' (verse 13).

If we take the parable outwardly, it suggests the need for alertness, so that when the Lord comes at the Last Day we shall be ready to receive him. The symbolism of the passage, however, fits inner reality more readily than it fits outer reality. Inwardly, the parable speaks of the approach of the kingdom from within. The kingdom is a wedding, a union of opposites, initiated by God. The bridegroom is the larger, Christlike personality who unites with the soul in the inner mystery of coming into selfhood. But the ego must be alert; that is, conscious. The lamps, which of course give out light, are symbols of the light of consciousness required of us if we are to enter into the kingdom. The final admonition, "stay awake," speaks directly to the need for continued consciousness of ourselves and of our relationship to the inner life. Events happen from within quite unexpectedly. One never knows what will be constellated within the inner depths, and when the great event of unification begins we must be prepared. There comes a time when it is too late, not because we are too old in years, but because we have languished so long in unconsciousness that our darkness is too great to be overcome.

This motif of being too late is often reflected in our dreams. We may arrive too late to catch the train as it leaves the station, or may find ourselves starting a journey but with the feeling of being far behind, or may have a great task set before us but feel overwhelmed because it is so late. There is a sense of timing to the inner life; something is to be accomplished within our earthly lifetime. This feeling of being too late can be exaggerated. No one who sincerely sets out on the inner way is too late. Although the ego is almost always behind the tempo of the inner life, persons even late in life may begin the inner journey. The only time it is truly too late is when the conscious personality is so rigid and solidified that the journey to the inner wedding never starts at all.

The wedding as the image of the kingdom is so central to Christianity that it prevailed in the early Church, where the supreme achievement of the Christian life was likened to the marriage of Christ, as bridegroom, to the Church or soul, as bride. The Song of Songs in the Old Testament, for instance, was interpreted by the early Fathers as a symbol of this inner mystery. Chastity was intended to bring about this union. Celibacy in the early Church was not originally directed against sexuality, but was intended to prepare the soul for the mystery of union with Christ. From this union would come the birth of Christ within the personality, bringing with it incorruptibility and freedom from evil, which is, psychologically speaking, totality. So the fourth-century bishop, Methodius, writes, "the Word, being stamped upon them (i.e., the faithful), and begotten in them by a true knowledge and faith, so in each one Christ is spiritually born. And, therefore, the Church swells and travails in birth until Christ is formed in us, so that each of the saints, by partaking of Christ, has been born a Christ" (Methodius, *Banquet of the Ten Virgins*, Chapter viii).

The image of the wedding is also prevalent in our dreams. When we begin to dream of weddings, it is usually a hopeful sign that a process of unification can begin, especially if the ego is not directly involved in the wedding. If the ego is one of the partners to the wedding, the dream may be talking of something else: perhaps possession, or seduction by certain aspects of the unconscious. There is also the great danger of inflation if the ego is too directly involved in the inner wedding. As in the parable, so in our dreams the role of the ego is to be conscious of the inner process. The wedding, as a union of opposites bringing about unification, characteristically occurs between figures other than that of the ego itself.

In addition to the wedding feast, there are many other representations of the kingdom which stress its unifying aspect. So Jesus says after the cure of the Centurion's servant,

> 'I tell you solemnly, nowhere in Israel have I found faith like this. And I tell you that many will come from east and west to take their places with Abraham and Isaac and Jacob at the feast in the kingdom of heaven' (Matthew 8:10–11).

Luke's version has,

> 'And men from east and west, from north and south, will come to take their places at the feast in the kingdom of God' (Luke 13:29).

Here the kingdom of heaven is shown as a great gathering together which includes all men. In Luke's version the gathering takes place from the four points of the compass. The image is that of a mandala, a concentric design featuring a quaternary or circular shape. Such concentric designs occur in religious symbolism throughout the world, and by the nature of their shape suggest wholeness or totality. The square is equal on all sides and so is in balance; the circle is the perfect shape, for all points are equidistant from the center. Such symbols are appropriate for the mystery of the kingdom, since their perfect structure suggests the wholeness and harmony of the kingdom of God. The Cross itself is such a symbol, and the early literature of Christianity speaks repeatedly of the mystery of the Cross. Its breadth and length, height and depth, embrace what is on the right and left and unite all in Christ, the Center.

A quotation from the Epistle to the Ephesians is instructive on this point where we read of Christ,

For he is the peace between us, and has made the two into
one and broken down the barrier which used to keep them
apart, actually destroying in his own person the hostility
caused by the rules and decrees of the Law. This was to
create one single New Man in himself out of the two of
them and by restoring peace through the cross, to unite
them both in a single Body and reconcile them with God
(Ephesians 2:14–16).

The reference here is outwardly to the union, through
Christ, of Jew and Gentile, but the image applies also to the
inner man. As long as we follow only the ethic of obedience, slavishly obeying some Law, we are divided within
ourselves. This is the "hostility caused by the rules and
decrees of the Law," for following the Law divides the
personality into one part, which will keep the Law, and
another part, which struggles against it. But Christ enables
the two parts of ourselves to become one New Man, for
through him it is possible for our two parts to confront
each other and accept each other. This act of consciousness
releases us from the Law and makes it possible for us to
follow the higher, synthesizing ethic of creativity.

The unity of the kingdom is a creative, not a static,
unity. It is not a peace of quiescence, but a creative inner
relatedness. God is primarily a Creator. He seeks to create
new life, and His kingdom generates a continual source of
new energies and possibilities. This is why, on an experiential level, no human being ever reaches the end of his inner
journey; for, as the kingdom begins to become a reality

within him, there is generated from within a host of new possibilities which his consciousness can fulfill. So the life of the kingdom is dynamic and continually evolving. This is the inner meaning of the story of the great catch of fish:

> [Jesus] said to Simon, 'Put out into deep water and pay out your nets for a catch'. 'Master,' Simon replied 'we worked hard all night long and caught nothing, but if you say so, I will pay out the nets.' And when they had done this they netted such a huge number of fish that their nets began to tear, so they signalled to their companions in the other boat to come and help them; when these came, they filled the two boats to sinking point (Luke 5:4–7).

Fish are a favorite symbol in our dreams for contents of the inner world. Fish lurk under the surface; they may be abundant but they are hard to see. However, they may be caught by patience and skill, and when they are caught they may be eaten and so taken into oneself. The contents of the inner world are also below the surface. They too may be lifted up into consciousness and taken as food for our lives.

Fish play an unusually important role in the New Testament. The disciples are fishermen; when Christ feeds the multitude it is with fish; a fish is miraculously caught to supply tax money when needed; fish is the food which Jesus eats after his resurrection. In the early Church Christ himself is likened to the fish, for the great fish is a symbol for the big content of the unconscious; that is, for totality. An ancient Christian author declares of this totality, "This stream of water [the fountain from God] sends forth the perennial stream of spirit, a stream containing but a single fish, taken with the hook of Divinity, and sustaining the whole world with its flesh as though it were in the sea." *

Creativity is a function of the inner imagination, not of the ego. The ego does not create out of itself but gives form and expression to the creativity which comes from within. An ego out of touch with the inner world can never be creative but only rigid, or can only mimic creativity. Creativity comes when we are in contact with the living contents of the inner world—the inner fish—and, bringing them to the surface, give them expression in life.

When one is in contact with the creative aspects of the inner world, one comes into possession of a vast treasure. There is no higher gift in life than the gift of creativity. Creativity is the expression of God's love and the greatest gift man can possess, for in the creatively led life we are acting in the image of God. This is the "heavenly treasure" of which Jesus speaks:

> 'Do not store up treasures for yourselves on earth, where moths and woodworms destroy them and thieves can break in and steal. But store up treasures for yourselves in heaven, where neither moth nor woodworms destroy them and thieves cannot break in and steal. For where your treasure is, there will your heart be also' (Matthew 6:19–21/Luke 12:33–34).

In the Bible, "heaven" does not refer to a geographical location but to spiritual reality. It is only our crude and materialistic outlook which insists on thinking of Biblical

* From *The Extant Writings of Julius Africanus.*

geography literally. The heavenly world, the world above, the angelic realm, is a way of referring to an aspect of the inner world. The treasures on earth refer to the attempt to accumulate outer material values, which are notoriously perishable and subject to destruction. The treasures in heaven are inner values, treasures of the spirit, a creative inner wealth, the gift of the kingdom, and these are imperishable. No outer calamity can take inner values from us, and if we seek after the inner creativity, our heart will be there also and so we will find God.

This same motif appears in our dreams, where we sometimes encounter a treasure. Coins may be found hidden in the ground, or a marvelous jewel may appear, or a large sum of money may come our way. These often refer to inner treasures with a spiritual or psychological value.

Because the man who seeks after the heavenly treasure will have his heart also in a heavenly search, this search is to be placed above everything else in life. Jesus, after referring to man's legitimate needs for material things, says,

'Set your hearts on his kingdom first, and on his righteousness, and all these other things will be given you as well' (Matthew 6:33).

Notice that it is not a matter of rejecting material things for the sake of spiritual ones. The material side of life is also necessary and important and is not to be despised. Rather, it is a matter of putting spiritual or psychological values first in our lives. Because there is always a secret connection between the inner and outer, the spiritual and material, the realization of spiritual values will result in a sufficiency of the material needs of life as well.

Frank was striving hard to find a happy life. He sought for this through his home and family, and worked with extraordinary diligence at a demanding job which took him away from home for long periods of time. But this was all right, for Frank was building his life. He was making good money, was pouring this into his beautiful house, with a pool and tennis court, and was creating for his attractive wife and children an ideal situation. It was enough for Frank to return home from time to time and feel the security of what he was creating. Then came the shock. His wife tired of him, of his way of life, and of the great demands placed upon her when he was home. She decided to throw Frank over, and in a few months Frank lost everything: wife, children, home, securities, all were gone. Frank was left alone with nothing but debts and memories on his hands. In this time of personal crisis Frank had to turn within. The outer values of his life had crumbled away; only if he could find inner values could he survive this terrible crisis. Frank's life has now become a search for the heavenly treasures. If he can find them, there will be no outer circumstance which will be able to separate him from God. Frank's life had been founded on sand, because he had lived so unconsciously, and had so completely identified his very soul with the outer things of his life instead of the inner things. Now he must find his soul within himself, and this will be a rock on which to build a new life. So Jesus is able to say,

'Therefore, everyone who listens to these words of mine and acts on them will be like a sensible man who built his house on rock. Rain came down, floods rose, gales blew and hurled themselves against that house, and it did not fall: it was founded on rock. But everyone who listens to these words of mine and does not act on them will be like a stupid man who built his house on sand. Rain came down, floods rose, gales blew and struck that house, and it fell; and what a fall it had!' (Matthew 7:24–27/Luke 6:47–49).

As we have mentioned, the "house" is the fabric of our life, the conscious orientation in which we live. A house founded on sand cannot withstand the rains, floods, and gales which come both from without and from within. Only a house founded on the rock of inner unity can withstand the destructive forces of life. Such a house built on rock is part of the legacy of the kingdom of God.

The coming of the kingdom represents the "end of the world," in the psychological sense that it is the end of an old order and the establishment of a new order of being. The creative contents of the inner world overthrow the previous organization of the personality. "Human" rule ends, and God's rule is made supreme in personality once the inner creativity flows into consciousness. The "complete man"—i.e., the Son of Man—is at the heart of this new person born into the kingdom of God. Because personality is the ultimately valuable thing in creation, since it is life's most unique expression, and because the kingdom is the goal of personality, the kingdom is futuristic and goal-centered. This aspect of the kingdom is depicted in apocalyptic language, as when Jesus describes the coming of the Son of Man:

'If, then, they say to you, "Look, he is in the desert", do not go there; "Look, he is in some hiding place", do not believe

it; because the coming of the Son of Man will be like
lightning striking in the east and flashing far into the west'
(Matthew 24:26–27/Luke 17:23–24).

Necessarily, the establishment of the kingdom brings
great insight. This is like lightning, an insight which bril-
liantly lights up the landscape of consciousness because it is
a knowledge from within. There have always been two
kinds of knowledge accessible to man: knowledge of the
outer, physical world, available through the methods of
science; and knowledge of inner things, religious knowledge which comes in the form of an inner "gnosis" * or
insight. It is knowledge through a personal experience of
the inner world, and is not universally accessible to everyone, but only to those to whom it has been revealed as they
have experienced inner reality. This inner, revealing gnosis
comes like lightning in the form of great insights into the
total meaning of things. It is founded not in reason or on
sensory experience, but on contact with an inner world
which *knows* dimensions and meanings to life not known
to the ordinary conscious state. When the Son of Man
comes, and the kingdom of God makes itself felt within,
this knowledges comes like a great flash of lightning.

Often our dreams pick up this same imagery, and a
person on the verge of a significant and revealing inner
experience may dream of a great flash of lightning which
illumines the sky. Or he may catch sight of a resplendent
mountain, or go on a mysterious journey under the sea on
some mission of great importance, or discover some myste-
riously significant object. There is a hunger in men for this

* A Greek word for knowledge of a personal or revealed kind.

kind of inner experience, a hunger which has too long been denied in our present time. Today we see a revolt against a one-sided extroverted attitude which cuts people off from their inner reality as many of our young people seek inner experience illicitly and dangerously through the use of drugs. A horrified society censures them, but must share the blame for having so denied inner reality that a starved generation seeks it chemically. So we have an ironic enigma: while many of the adult population try to keep from having an inner experience through tranquilizing drugs, many of the younger population try to have an inner experience through "mind-expanding" drugs. The only healthy way is to let our own God-given inner reality find expression in natural ways.

Most men live only on the level of outer reality. The inner world is so strange to consciousness that the bulk of mankind ignores its existence. When the inner world does burst upon us it comes as a great surprise.

'As it was in Noah's day, so will it be when the Son of Man comes. For in those days before the Flood people were eating, drinking, taking wives, taking husbands, right up to the day Noah went into the ark, and they suspected nothing till the Flood came and swept all away. It will be like this when the Son of Man comes. Then of two men in the fields one is taken, one left; of two women at the millstone grinding, one is taken, one left' (Matthew 24:37–41/Luke 17:26–27, 34–35).

One may well imagine that Noah's neighbors thought him a fool for building his Ark in the midst of dry land; only Noah was convinced of the imminence of the Flood.

So with regard to the inner world, most people think that those who take it seriously are fools to concern themselves with such nonsense. When the kingdom finally does burst upon men it catches them by surprise, and only the few are able to come into relationship with the inner reality.

The analogy with the Flood is most appropriate since water, in the form of the ocean, rivers, floods, torrents, streams, or pools, is a favorite symbol for inner reality; it is *the* symbol par excellence for the origin of our psychic life.

Because of the suddenness with which inner reality may burst upon us, an attitude of wakefulness is required of us. Inner reality is beyond our control. We cannot predict or control the inner realm any more than we can predict and control our dreams. We can only be conscious and seek to be prepared to understand. So Jesus says,

> 'So stay awake, because you do not know the day when your master is coming. . . . Therefore, you too must stand ready because the Son of Man is coming at an hour you do not expect' (Matthew 24:42,44/Luke 12:39–40).

When the Son of Man does come, when inner reality does burst in upon consciousness, it brings with it a reorganization of the personality so violent and complete that it can be described only in apocalyptic images. Whether this reorganization takes place very swiftly or over a long period of time under the continued impact on consciousness of the kingdom within, the result is still the same: the old attitudes and structures of the personality must give way to new ones. This is vividly portrayed by Jesus in words such as the following:

'Immediately after the distress of those days the sun will be darkened, the moon will lose its brightness, the stars will fall from the sky and the powers of heaven will be shaken. And then the sign of the Son of Man will appear in heaven; then too all the peoples of the earth will beat their breasts; and they will see the Son of Man coming on the clouds of heaven with power and great glory. And he will send his angels with a loud trumpet to gather his chosen from the four winds, from one end of heaven to the other' (Matthew 24:29–31/Luke 21:25–27/Mark 13:24–27).

Dreams frequently occur in which the heavenly bodies play a major role. We dream of the sun or moon, or find ourselves gazing up into a brilliant starry night. The heavenly bodies refer to the archetypal contents of the inner world, the dominant psychic forces which powerfully influence consciousness. The image of the Son of Man appearing in heaven is not to be taken geographically. It is the inner heaven where the Son of Man, the archetype of completeness, will be found. When he manifests himself in the personality, there is a gathering together from the four winds. Here we have again the image of a mandala, the quaternity, the gathering into a unity of all the aspects of the hitherto fragmented self.

Another way in which the mystery of the coming of the kingdom is expressed is in the image of the Undivided Man. Unity is the goal of the kingdom. Since the primary division in a human being is the masculine-feminine division, a primary symbol of the kingdom is that of the wedding, as we have seen. In a wedding male and female unite in one. From an external point of view this is only a sexual union, made possible by physical intercourse. From the psychological point of view the sexual act itself is an image of a higher unity which can take place within the individual as the diverse parts of himself become one with each other. This is why St. Paul says,

> 'For this reason, a man must leave his father and mother and be joined to his wife, and the two will become one body. *This mystery has many implications;* but I am saying it applies to Christ and the Church' (Ephesians 5:31–32; italics mine).

Or, as the King James version puts it,

> 'This is a great mystery.'

The mystery to which St. Paul refers is the mystery of the undivided, or androgynous, man, a man in whom division has been replaced by unity. No human being is pure masculinity or femininity, but each person contains elements of both. A man usually identifies with his masculine side, and his feminine side becomes unconscious to him, so that his unconscious carries a feminine sign. A woman usually identifies with her feminine side, so that her unconscious carries a masculine figure who represents her unconscious masculine component. The union of masculine and feminine is therefore the symbol for the union of the psyche, and the image of the marriage is, naturally, the primary representation of this inner mystery.

The myth of the androgynous, undivided man has long

haunted man's mind. Plato in his "Symposium" tells the myth of the original man who was round and then was split in two to form male and female. The Book of Genesis hints at it in the story of Adam, out of whose side Eve was taken. The early Church contained the symbol in its image of the mystical union between Christ and his Church, of which the Song of Songs, with its vivid love imagery, was regarded as a symbol. Mystical theology has long talked of the mystery of the androgyne, especially in the Kabbala, in the philosophy of Jacob Boehme, in alchemy, and in the mystical experience of the saints of the Church, where it is referred to as the inner spiritual marriage.*

It is not surprising to find that Jesus also knows of the mystery of the Undivided Man. This is what underlies his reply to the Sadducees about marriage in the afterlife:

'You are wrong, because you understand neither the scriptures nor the power of God. For at the resurrection men and women do not marry; no, they are like the angels in heaven' (Matthew 22:29–30/Mark 12:24–25).

Or, as we find it in Luke,

'The children of this world take wives and husbands, but those who are judged worthy of a place in the other world and in the resurrection from the dead do not marry because

* See for instance Evelyn Underhill's *Mysticism*, pages 137, 335. Modern writers such as Nicholas Berdyaev and Herman Hesse also hint at this supreme mystery (cf. Berdyaev's *The Meaning of the Creative Act*, pages 63–65 and 175–176, and Hesse's *Damian*). Berdyaev writes, "Androgynity is the ultimate union of male and female in a higher God-like being, the ultimate conquest of decadence and strife, the restoration in man of the image and likeness of God" (*The Meaning of the Creative Act*, page 207).

they can no longer die, for they are the same as the angels, and being children of the resurrection they are sons of God' (Luke 20:34–36).

Death comes through division. The men of the resurrection are those who belong to the kingdom. In them an indivisible man has been forged by God's power and man's becoming conscious. In such men the male and female are one; that is, the disparate parts of the personality have found their union together. By virtue of this such a person is a "son of God."

In the apocryphal Gospel According to Thomas, there are other sayings of Jesus with this same motif. Jesus said,

> When you make the two one, you shall become sons of Man (Logion 106)

and

> When you make the two one, and you make the inner as the outer and the outer as the inner and the above as the below, and when you make the male and female into a single one, so that the male will not be male and the female will not be female . . . then shall you enter the Kingdom (Logion 22).

The opposite sides of personality are so different that only a great force can draw them together in union. This power is love. Love is a stronger power than the forces of disunion. In love even the opposites can become one, and their differences unite in one indivisible whole. This is why love is the strongest power there is, stronger than sin, or death, or evil, as Christ showed on the Cross, where he demonstrated the triumphant qualities of love. This is also why it is said that God Himself is love. It is not surprising, then, to find that, where love occurs in human relationships, the image of the Undivided Man is also spontaneously present, and that such a love has an enormously healing capacity.

This kind of uniting, healing love is visible in the phenomenon known as the "transference." While the term "transference" is a technical term deriving from psychotherapy, it is actually a psychological event which can occur between two people under widely varying circumstances. Usually existing between a man and a woman, it is characterized by very strong erotic feelings, often with sexual overtones. In psychotherapy both counselor and counselee may be aware of the existence of such feelings in the counseling situation. It may also occur between a patient and his doctor, a student and his teacher, a married man and the "other woman," or between two young people, in which case it is referred to as "falling in love." The love which exists between the two people *is* love. But to the extent that they are not aware of each other as individual human beings, with all the faults and frailties of human beings, but are seeing in each other only idealized images, the love is not personal but "divine." Its source is the enormous attraction of the opposites which is constellated in the transference phenomenon. This is a different thing than one human being's coming to know, respect, and love the personality of another human being.

If the transference phenomenon is handled uncon-

sciously, it will turn out badly. The John and Mary who
fall madly in love, which means they project on each other
their own idealized images and feel the enormous pull of
the opposites to unite, characteristically fall violently out of
love again in a short time. This is no accident. In order for a
conscious development to take place in such people, rather
than their simply being immersed in the sea of unconscious
love, it will be necessary that they recognize both their
own individuality and the individuality of the other person.
To do this, each must be driven apart from the other in
order to differentiate. Uncannily the unconscious will find
a way to produce quarrels between them in order to facili-
tate this separation. Since the disappointment in each other
now becomes very great, the earlier love easily turns to
hate and disillusionment. Only if John and Mary can come
to see the inner meaning of their relationship, and so bring
it to a higher level of consciousness, can it hope to last. But
in this case the union of opposites will have to take place in
the development of the personality of each of them, and
not as a mystique unconsciously drawing them together.

In all cases the danger is always the tendency on the part
of those involved in this kind of love to concretize sexually
the emotions they feel. They are driven by the supreme
image of the kingdom of God, the image of the wedding;
but as long as they are unconscious of this image, they may
be compulsively drawn into a sexual relationship. Then the
inner meaning of the experience is lost, because sexuality
under these conditions is a regression to an unconscious,
nonindividual event, since sexuality without psychological
consciousness is generic and not individual. Should this
occur in a professional context, the result is ruinous to the

psychological development of both doctor or therapist and patient. Should it occur in an attraction outside of marriage, the result may be equally ruinous, for a man or a woman who gives way to this may not only leave behind him or her a ruined home and an unredeemed guilt, but fall prey to his or her most unconscious side.

The solution is to hold within oneself, and within the context of the relationship, all the affects, desires, feelings, and aspirations. The individual then becomes a crucible containing the elements of totality, and the intense feelings are like a heat which brings these elements through a process and into completion. The image of the kingdom as a wedding feast then works within all parties concerned, affecting them in the innermost levels of their being.

While the man-woman transference is the most common example of this divine love, another form of the transference must also be mentioned: the transference which can take place between a man and a youth. The figure of the Androgyne can be represented as a divine youth. Christ himself in the early Church was likened frequently to a brilliant and shining youth; in this form he was often said by the early Christians to appear in dreams. The youth embodies within himself both masculine and feminine aspects of his personality and by his strength and connection to life carries the image of totality. Berdyaev writes, "Only a virgin-boy, a man-androgyne, is the image and likeness of God." *

In ancient times there was no particular stigma attached to the love of a man for a youth. A good example of such a

---

* *Meaning of the Creative Act*, page 65.

deep love and affection, for instance, is found in *Hadrian's Memoirs*, in which the Roman Emperor Hadrian's deep love for a young man, who obviously carried both masculine and feminine personality components, is shown, In our modern day, however, any erotic feelings aroused in a man for another man would be frightening because of our exaggerated cultural fear of homosexuality. Such emotions are not homosexuality but homoeroticism and occur in many men who are sexually well oriented. Repression of these feelings leads to repression of much that is valuable and desirable in a man. Acting them out, on the other hand, leads to guilt and unconsciousness and a negative enslavement to sexuality. It is possible, however, for a man to recognize that his feeling for another man is his longing for the Androgyne, a reflection of the deep desire to realize the union of opposites within himself, and to feel the reality of this greatest of archetypes as the foundation of his own being.

We have come a long way since we first began to look at the meaning of the kingdom of God in Jesus' thought. The outline of a psychological-spiritual theory of the kingdom of God has been drawn. According to this view Jesus had in mind a uniquely personal state of being, potentially open to all people, but to which only a few will be conscious enough to respond. Those who enter will have to shed their masks and confront their inner enemies. The ethic of those who want to enter the kingdom will be a creative ethic founded on consciousness of oneself.

The road to the kingdom will be an inner road, a way of the soul, in which a man becomes increasingly connected to his inner world. Nothing can be excluded which belongs to man's wholeness. In the kingdom, body, soul, and spirit, sexuality, eros, and meaning—all are part of totality. The final entrance into the kingdom subordinates consciousness to a great reality within. Creativity enters into the personality, shaking the old personality structure with apocalyptic power, and establishing a new personality not dominated by a narrow ego-consciousness but by God Himself, for this new personality is creative and God is a Creator.

Since creativity comes from unity, and unity comes from a drawing together of opposites, the well-spring of the kingdom is love, for love alone can unite disparate things into one. With this spiritual theory of the kingdom of God in mind, it remains now to look back once more at the personality and mission of Jesus, with a view to the meaning of Jesus Christ for a Christianity which belongs to the future as well as to the past.

Conclusion

Christianity—

A Religion

for a Modern Era

✠✠✠

Jesus of Nazareth was the first individual man, the first man sufficiently conscious that he was not divided against himself, not contained in a collective psychology. Like the great Hebrew prophets of the Old Testament, he was directly in contact with the numinosum of God. Unlike them, he saw the meaning of God's purpose for the life of the individual as well as for the life of the nation. It is his stress on individual development, individual consciousness, and individual relatedness to God and man in this earthly life which makes him an entirely new figure in religious history.

He is the prototype both of the developed ego and of the Total Man. On the road to the Cross he is the uniquely individual ego, made strong by consciousness and connection to God. Jesus, assuming the burden of crucifixion voluntarily and willingly, is the human ego at its prime, but on the Cross Jesus manifests more than the ego alone. Here he reveals totality, and is seen to be the "Son of Man." *By*

his suffering, his death and resurrection, he merges forever
with the human psyche, and becomes the archetype of
totality for all of us, transforming the destiny of
mankind.

One thing which traditional Christianity has lacked up
until now is a philosophy of the future. The early Christians generally supposed that the world would soon end.
They were still caught in the conventional thinking of their
times and did not fully comprehend the dynamic new
psychological developments for man made possible by
Jesus Christ. As a result Christian theology has never developed a philosophy of the future or, consequently, a theology of the workings of the Holy Spirit.

What such a Christian philosophy of the future might be
is suggested by the findings of the sciences of evolution and
psychology. In studying the human embryo, it can be
determined that the fetus undergoes in the nine months of
gestation a process of physical evolution analogous to the
evolutionary development of the human body over
hundreds of thousands of years. Similarly, the human
psyche has also evolved from a more primitive adaptation,
in which the ego was relatively undeveloped, to a relatively
sophisticated state. Eric Neumann has traced these evolutionary stages of the development of consciousness in his
book *The Origins and History of Consciousness;* he has
shown that man's mythologies the world over contain the
story of the development of man's psychological life.
Today, in the psychological development of the individual,
the ego undergoes a process of psychic evolution analogous
to that of the race, to the point where mythlike dreams
occur at typical stages on the way of this development.

Man has undergone a process of physical and psychological evolution which has brought him to his present point of development.

In Jesus of Nazareth we see this process of development at an apex. In him, human consciousness reached a uniquely complete and individual stage. By virtue of this unique development and his subsequent death and Resurrection, the way has been paved for man to develop as never before. Until Jesus' time psychological development was primarily accomplished on a collective basis. It was the herd, the group, the nation, the people, who were the bearers of human growth. Since Jesus, it has been the individual who carries forward the evolution of man; and the forward thrust of the creative life power, which is God's Holy Spirit in the world, takes place through the development of conscious life and the integration and completion of the total man.

Christianity for a modern era must take into account the psychological dimension. Even as Jesus became a complete man, so our calling is to imitate him, not by mimicking what we suppose to have been his virtues, but by approximating completeness ourselves as much as is possible. In this way we manifest Christ within us. We can then say that the Christ child is born again in our life, that the purpose of God in creating us is being fulfilled. Christianity is the most psychological of all religions because of this emphasis which it places on the inner development of the individual and the important role which it assigns to the ego as the bearer of consciousness.

Such an emphasis would incur the danger of becoming a narrowly selfish concern were it not that our fulfillment as persons requires our participation in the life and needs of others. For completeness to occur in the life of an individual, he must be involved in the totality of life. Becoming a complete person is a matter of psychological development, but not of psychologizing. Totality comes when life is lived completely, when the demands of both inner and outer realities are met consciously. No man can hope to find his own salvation without being deeply concerned with the salvation of others, for man is complete in relationship and not as an island.

The kingdom of God is a personal, psychologically real experience, but it is not a purely personal experience. It always has a transcendental character as well as an immediate character. The kingdom does not belong to us; we belong to the kingdom. In seeking for the establishment of the kingdom within our personalities, we do not reduce the kingdom to a narrow, personal dimension. Rather, we come to belong to a broad, transcendental dimension. What the kingdom is in itself can never be contained by rational consciousness but can be expressed only in symbols. It cannot be *thought*, but can only be embraced, perhaps for a moment, in mystical experience, for it far transcends personal consciousness and the limitations of the ego's thinking.

In its transcendence the kingdom is a call into the future. In grounding our lives upon the kingdom within, we become a part of the evolving consciousness of man, which means being part of God's intention for man. Here, in the evolution of consciousness, taking place through individuals but always transcending the individual in its significance, is the Christianity of the future.

⊕

Bibliography

✤✤✤

Berdyaev, Nicholas, *The Destiny of Man*. A Harper Torchbook, New York: Harper & Row, Publishers, Inc., 1960.
———, *The Meaning of the Creative Act*. A Collier Book. New York: The Macmillan Company, 1962.
Edinger, Edward F., "Christ as Paradigm of the Individuation Ego." *Spring* magazine, 1966 (published by The Analytical Psychology Club of New York, 130 E. 39th St., Suite 306, New York, N. Y. 10016).
Jung, C. G., *Aion*. Collected Works, Vol. 9, Part 2. New York: Pantheon Books, 1951.
———, *Memories, Dreams, Reflections*. A Pantheon Book. New York: Random House, Inc., 1961. (Also in paperback: Vintage, V268, Random House.)
———, *Psychology and Religion: West and East*. Collected Works, Vol. II. New York: Pantheon Books, 1958.
Kelsey, Morton T., *Dreams: The Dark Speech of the Spirit*. New York: Doubleday & Company, Inc., 1968.
———, *Tongue Speaking: An Experiment in Spiritual Experience*. New York: Doubleday & Company, Inc., 1964. (Also in paperback: Waymark W16, Doubleday.)
Kunkel, Fritz, *Creation Continues*. New York: Charles Scribner's Sons, 1947.
———, *In Search of Maturity*. New York: Charles Scribner's Sons, 1943.
Phillips, Dorothy, *The Choice Is Always Ours*, rev. ed. New York: Harper & Row, Publishers, Inc., 1960.

Pillai, K. C., *Light Through an Eastern Window.* New York: Robert Speller & Sons, Publishers, Inc., 1963.

Sanford, John A., *Dreams: God's Forgotten Language.* Philadelphia: J. B. Lippincott Company, 1968.

Index

❖❖❖

222